Maverick Lineage

What I Learned about Black Conservatism in America

Philip Blackett

To my grandfather, Frank Wilson Wade, who stepped in to help raise me when I was growing up. You taught me what it means to be a man, Biblically speaking, and how to be confident in your own skin and unintimidated with your own voice, regardless of what others had to say in response. You prepared me to stand unapologetically strong for God, for my family, and for my country during the challenging times we live in today.

***

To the men of the past and present who inspired, guided, and challenged me on what it means to be conservative, and thus a maverick, within the Black community today: Frederick Douglass, Hiram Rhodes Revels, Booker T. Washington, George Washington Carver, Thomas Sowell, Colin Powell, Herman Cain, Walter E. Williams, J.C. Watts, Dr. Ben Carson, Larry Elder, Tim Scott, Shelby Steele, and Jason L. Riley. I thank you for your unflinching resolve to stay committed to conservative principles, despite societal pressures, and the example you lived courageously that I hope to carry on and model for the next generation with a commitment to God, to family, and to country.

Preface

"I cannot understand people who say that minorities should be represented everywhere and yet are upset when there are blacks represented in the conservative movement." – Thomas Sowell

As I lay this meditative pathway before you, know that it is more than a historical treatise or a mere collection of ideologies. This book stands as an exploration of courage, faith, and enduring principles that have quietly shaped a segment of American society often overlooked by the mainstream narrative – the Black Conservative movement.

The purpose of crafting these pages was born from a dual imperative. **Firstly, to help unveil the rich legacy of one of the most misunderstood and misrepresented groups in American political thought; and secondly, to engage in meaningful dialogue and foster insight that transcends the binary constructs frequently imposed upon American politics.**

Charged with a mission to *Grow God's People, Grow God's Business-es, and Grow God's Kingdom*, the core of my identity has always been my relationship with the Lord and to be a good and faithful steward of all that He has entrusted me with in my lifetime. Each of us is a steward of the essence of divine teachings, to interact with the world not as passive observers but as dynamic shapers of our collective destinies.

Drawing from Biblical principles and aligning with my faith-driven worldview, I engaged in countless discussions with individuals from diverse backgrounds. I have candidly witnessed the frustration and yearning for knowledge amongst young scholars – determined yet disillusioned students grappling with the single-story, simplistic portrayal of Black political thought. This ignited in me the need to articulate a broader spectrum, not just for my own understanding, but to enliven the discourse with tales of a resilient philosophical stance steeped in tradition yet invigoratingly contemporary and frankly growing in momentum today.

Gratitude extends to the numerous scholars, historians, and everyday heroes whose stories and indomitable spirits have emboldened this narrative. The voices of men and women who have navigated this quiet revolution have not just inspired this book; they are its backbone.

To the attentive eyes that grace these words, your investment of time and spirit humbles me. With an enthusiasm shared among peers, I hope to usher you into a more profound understanding, and perhaps challenge your perspectives – without a hint of arrogance, but with the shared excitement of discovering uncharted waters together.

As we engage in this reading journey together, let it be known that no prior expertise in the fields of political science or African American studies is required, though an open mind and a desire to delve beyond superficial interpretations and media commentary are essential.

This book humbly aims to conquer misconceptions and present more of the truth about Black Conservatism in an approachable, compelling style that feels as comfortable as a dialogue with a mentor or friend. The text is founded on experienced wisdom, presented with clarity and the drive of an instructive voice that offers not just facts, but visions and aspirations of what could be.

In closing, thank you for embarking on this journey through the pages I have laid out with care and purpose. **I acknowledge that I do not know everything about this subject, yet I share with you what I have learned, while also acknowledging that I continue to be a student in this topic.** May the solutions and understandings you seek be found in the legacy, debate, and predictions herein. Turn forth, explore confidently, and allow the spectrum of Black Conservatism to reveal its vibrant hues to a watchful eye and an expectant heart. Let's get started.

Contents

Chapter One

Beyond the Monolith: Defying Political Stereotypes

T he midday sun stretched over the tree-lined avenues of Washington, D.C., casting long shadows that mimicked the silent pondering of Jeremiah as he walked. The scents of autumn melded with the distant clamor of city life — each a whispering thread in the fabric of his thoughts. His hands, seasoned by years of turning the pages of spiritual texts and crafting campaign strategies, slid into the pocket of his tailored suit.

Jeremiah recalled the vivid discussions at the last community roundtable; a tapestry of Black voices rising with conservative principles, voices often hushed in the grand narrative of American politics. A young woman had spoken, her words a dance of passion and intellect, breathlessly articulating the storied resilience woven into the lineage which bent but never broke beneath the relentless winds of change. She represented a history too seldom recounted — a history where conservative values in Black political identities were as intricate and foundational as the stars in the sky.

As he strode through the city, Jeremiah's mind marinated in the ceaseless ambition that drove him. He carried with him the proverbs of Solomon, the calculated resolve of Nehemiah rebuilding the walls, and the economic intelligence of modern theorists. It was a symphony of wisdom that guided him through negotiations, inspired trust in potential investors, and breathed life into his entrepreneurial dreams.

Yet his heart weighed heavy with the misconception, as persistent as the marble monuments around him, that each Black hand raised in America bore indelible liberal blue ink. How, he wondered, could the nuanced spectrum of Black thought be gracefully scribed into the consciousness of a nation that seemed to look only for uniformity? His purpose had germinated in this very tension — the calling to unveil the diversity of conviction, thought and belief seated at the often unseen and often ridiculed table of Black conservatism.

He paused, looking up at an oak tree standing sentinel against the sky, its leaves a golden canvas painted by the changing season. He saw every leaf as a story, a life, a choice that refracted through the prism of freedom — each falling in its own time, on its own path. He had been like them once, unsure of where his descent might land him, but in its certainty, he found kinship with the roots that stretched deep and unseen, anchoring the towering presence above.

"How then," Jeremiah thought, anchoring himself in the now as he extended his vision beyond the forthcoming elections and into the horizon of a lifetime's work, "shall we write this new chapter?" Not as a chronicle of echoes, but as a living dialogue that engaged and embraced the multiplicity of voices calling for recognition and for realization, not only of their individual goals but also of the aspirations of the communities they live in and serve - even if those residents don't accept them as part of their own.

The resonance of footsteps on the sidewalk became a metaphor to him: the solitary journey, amidst a collective march, toward a horizon of understanding where the sun's rays illuminated each path with equal ardor. The air was brisk as the day waned, and across the streets, the leaves rustled, whispering in agreement — an audience of nature to the unfolding narrative of human endeavor.

Do these winds of change hold the promise to uplift the leaves of long-held misconceptions, to let them touch the ground of reality, symbolizing the fertile growth of a more nuanced understanding of Black political thought and identity in America?

Unveiling the Spectrum Within Us

The tapestry of American political thought unveils a particularly intricate thread when one examines the patterns of Black conservatism. To embark on a journey through the untold spectrum of conservatism is not just an academic endeavor but a spiritual pilgrimage to the heart of Black patriotism. This chapter lays the cornerstone for a profound exploration into the multifaceted identities of Black conservatives, their historical roots, and the vibrant tableau of ideologies that they represent. By examining the pages of history, spirituality, and entrepreneurship within Black conservatism, we aim to recognize the values that have kept this movement robust in the face of substantial challenges.

The misnomer that equates Black political identity exclusively with liberal ideologies is about to be dismantled. Let us begin by recognizing that Black conservative thought itself does not exist as a monolith; it thrives as a spectrum. From the pews of the church where faith intertwines with policy, to the businesses where economic pragmatism prevails, the tenets of this conservatism run deep. As a beacon of self-determination, traditional family values, and fiscal responsibility, Black conservatism's roots are as historical as they are topical — sometimes invoking the wisdom of Scripture, at other times calling for entrepreneurial strength.

Understanding the historical narrative of Black conservatism requires a look back at the figures who paved the way with their intellectual rigor and moral fortitude. The life lessons of pioneers such as Booker T. Washington and Frederick Douglass impart timeless wisdom on the values of self-reliance and education as tools of empowerment. Their teachings resonate within contemporary Black conservative thought, reminding us that the solution to current adversities often lie in the persistence and innovation of the past.

Defying political stereotypes, the Black conservative thought espouses a pragmatic approach to social and economic challenges, frequently utilizing strategies born from real-world experiences. This chapter brings forth stories that echo the entrepreneurial spirit, where Black conservatives have used their business acumen not just for personal success, but as testimonies of a broader political ideology that prizes industry and innovation. Each narrative serves as a building block for understanding the allure of conservative principles among Black communities.

These conservative values are manifested in diverse ways across American society, influencing debates on education, economic policy, and social issues. Recognizing the contributions of Black conservatives to these areas of discourse provides a clearer perspective on their role in shaping policy and public opinion. It is fundamental to understand the historical evolution of Black conservative ideology to appreciate its current and future trajectories.

Moreover, within the spiritual realm, Black conservatism often draws upon scriptural guidance to reinforce its social and moral philosophies. Proverbs and biblical parables often intersect with policy, giving this intellectual tradition a faith-based foundation that speaks to its adherents. This chapter will explain how sacred texts inform and inspire the Black conservative viewpoint, grounding political notions in spiritual conviction.

In keeping with the entrepreneurial spirit, this discourse will also challenge readers to actively engage with the content, not just as passive consumers but as critical thinkers eager to reshape their understanding of American political diversity. Encouraged to probe deeper and think broader, readers will gain more than just historical knowledge; they will equip themselves with insights that provoke action and foster resilience in political thought and discourse. After reading this book, they may find themselves more conservative than they originally thought.

Through this exploration, one can better grasp the rich contributions of Black conservatives to American political culture and predict how they might continue to influence the trajectory of our national discourse. In honoring the past and anticipating the future, we uncover not just shades of Black patriotism but the vibrant spectrum of an oft-misunderstood segment of American civic life.

The narrative of Black conservatism in America is richly embroidered with a myriad of threads, each depicting a unique stance within the political tapestry. It is perhaps too simplistic to view Black political thought as a monolith – indeed, it is as varied and dynamic as the community from which it emanates. Intellectual leaders, community activists, and political figures from within the Black community have, for generations, embraced conservative principles ranging from self-reliance and family values to skepticism about the role of government in personal lives.

The robust voices within Black conservative thought are often overshadowed by a prevailing assumption that equates Black identity inherently with progressive politics. Yet, historical evidence and contemporary expressions reveal a different truth: Black Americans have found resonance in conservative ideologies, including economic self-sufficiency, Judeo-Christian values, and the prioritization of education. These ideas have served as cornerstones for numerous influential Black leaders and thinkers who have shaped not only Black history but also the broader American political landscape.

Faith is an integral facet of Black conservatism, with many adherents drawing deeply from spiritual wells. The core beliefs within many spiritual teachings – such as the emphasis on personal virtue, community service, and a strong nuclear family structure – are reflected in the conservative values upheld by many within the community. As such, faith-based principles have crafted a foundation upon which many Black conservatives stand, influencing debates on policy and informing their political engagement.

Entrepreneurial endeavors within the Black community also mirror conservative sentiments, celebrating and harnessing the power of the free markets. The drive to foster economic growth through business ownership, job creation and financial literacy has been an enduring battle cry for many Black conservatives. This commitment to economic empowerment is not merely theoretical; it is lived out in the thriving businesses and financial ventures initiated and sustained by Black entrepreneurs who not only seek personal success but also aim to uplift their communities.

The seasoned expertise of Black individuals in various economic spheres demonstrates this conservative principle in action. Through tales of overcoming adversity, building successful enterprises, and advocating for policies that foster economic freedom, Black conservatives underscore the merit of self-reliance and the potential for individual prosperity within a capitalist framework. These narratives serve as practical blueprints, mentoring and inspiring others to pursue similar paths to economic autonomy and financial independence.

Shattering the One-Dimensional Perspective

When engaging with Black political thought, it is essential to adopt a listening posture, one that is both patient and devoid of preconceived notions. Engaging with the lived experiences of Black conservatives provides a more nuanced understanding of why and how conservative values resonate within segments of the Black community. It is a dialogue that requires more than just casual acknowledgment; it demands a comprehensive exploration of the cultural, economic, and spiritual underpinnings that inform these political beliefs.

Despite the complexities of their perspectives, **Black conservatives are often met with skepticism both within and outside the Black community. There is a prevailing communal doubt over the authenticity of their "blackness" and a shared misconception that a conservative viewpoint is inexorably at odds with the fight for racial equality and justice.** Yet, what is often overlooked is the diversity in how Black conservatives approach these very issues – advocating for solutions that are rooted in empowerment, accountability, and self-determination.

The Roots of Black Conservatism

The genesis of conservative principles within Black political identities can be traced back to the period following the abolition of slavery. At this pivotal moment, many African Americans, steeped in the ethical teachings of spiritual texts, turned to self-reliance and the pursuit of economic independence as cornerstones for empowerment. These values resonated with the conservative tenets of personal responsibility and limited government intervention. Historic figures such as **Booker T. Washington** championed this philosophy, arguing that economic progress and education, rather than immediate political integration, were the most effective avenues for African American advancement.

Faith as a Guiding Principle

The moral fortitude necessary for such an endeavor was often derived from deep spiritual roots. These individuals found solace and strength in the scriptural promises that spoke of hope, perseverance and justice. Faith communities played an instrumental role in promoting conservative values, emphasizing hard work, integrity, and family structure. The teachings of revered spiritual leaders were interwoven with the principles of conservatism, providing a faith-driven foundation that sustained Black communities through the trials of segregation and racial discrimination.

A Growing Entrepreneurial Spirit

Embodying the entrepreneurial spirit, Black conservatives sought to leverage capitalism for individual, family and community upliftment.

They invested in businesses, acquired property, and placed a strong emphasis on economic self-sufficiency. This aligns with modern conservative principles that highlight the importance of free market economies as a pathway to success. By fostering entrepreneurship, they provided tangible examples of how conservative ideology could be put into practice to achieve progress and create generational wealth.

Practical Wisdom from Past Experiences

The teachings of past leaders remain relevant today, offering practical wisdom gleaned from real-world experiences. Their lives are testaments to the value of perseverance and dedication in the face of systemic barriers. By grounding their approach in the tangible realities of the business world, they illustrate the enduring applicability of conservative principles in forging paths to success for many African Americans.

Public Policy and Self-Determination

On a policy level, Black conservatism has often expressed a preference for strategies that enhance self-determination. **Vouching for educational choice, community-led development, and welfare reform, these political stances reflect a commitment to fostering environments where individuals can thrive without excessive governmental dependency.** This stance, though sometimes misconstrued, is rooted in a desire for equitable opportunity and the autonomy to make decisions that best serve one's self, family and community.

Resilience in the Face of Adversity

The journey of Black conservatives is one of incredible resilience. It paints a picture of a demographic steadfast in its convictions, even when these ideals buck the expectations of the dominant political narratives. Personal anecdotes of overcoming prejudice and surmounting obstacles underscore this resilience, offering guidance and motivation for those who walk in their footsteps.

Broadening the Spectrum of Political Thought

The spectrum of Black political thought is not monolithic, and to presume so is to disregard the rich tapestry of diverse opinions and ideologies within the community. By integrating a broad range of insights from various fields, the multifaceted nature of Black conservative thinking is revealed. Economics, theology, and political strategy all play a part in shaping a worldview that is both reflective and forward-thinking, contributing to a nuanced understanding of conservative values within the context of Black America.

Dialogue and Understanding

Engaging in constructive dialogue is critical for understanding the historic and current landscape of Black conservatism. With respect, humility and openness, we can uncover the myriad of reasons why conservative principles resonate within segments of the Black community. Understanding is not gained through assumption, but through active listening and the genuine exchange of ideas—much like a mentor imparts wisdom to a student eager to learn.

The Importance of Narrative

Finally, as we strive to appreciate the historical nuances of Black conservative thought, the power of narrative cannot be understated. By telling the stories of those who espouse these beliefs, we offer a correction to the one-dimensional narrative often portrayed in the mainstream media.

The understanding of Black political thought has long been confined within a limited scope, often restricted to aligning with liberal ideologies. This notion, deep-rooted in the American political narrative, does not withstand the scrutiny of history and present-day realities. The truth is that Black political thought precludes simplistic categorizations; it is as nuanced and varied as the community from which it springs.

The Spiritual Lens of Conservatism

Drawing upon the spiritual principles that have fortified countless individuals through the ages, Black conservatism in many aspects harnesses these tenets. Religious teachings and texts have provided a moral compass, admittedly influencing ideologies across the political spectrum, but particularly resonating with **conservative values such as family unity, personal responsibility, and a reverence for life. Black Americans, many deeply connected to their faith, often find that conservative principles echo their religious convictions, not as an antithesis to progress, but as its very foundation.**

It's essential to approach the discussion of Black conservatism not as a paradox but as a legitimate expression of a community's complexity. Personal anecdotes crystallize this point — there exist within Black communities elders who preach the merit of hard work and the importance of tradition, values that are harmonized with conservatism. These stories exemplify a lived experience that blurs the purported clear line between liberalism and conservatism for Black Americans.

The historical development of conservatism within Black communities alludes to numerous motivations for conservative leanings — motivations that arise from real-world experiences and pragmatic considerations.

In discussions surrounding Black political thought, it is vital to integrate insights from various fields like economics and theology, recognizing that these disciplines inform one another. For instance, economic empowerment and self-sufficiency have a theological underpinning in many Black churches, advocating for a life free from dependence on external systems — a fundamental conservative principle. Case studies of Black-owned businesses thriving under free-market policies reinforce the efficacy and appeal of conservative economic ideologies.

Appreciating The Diversity of Black Voices

Empowerment stems from recognizing the diversity of voices and experiences within the Black community. **Highlighting the achievements of Black conservatives in politics, academia, and business inspires motivation and perseverance. These stories counter the misconception that to be Black is to be liberal**, revealing an array of perspectives that are often muted within mainstream political dialogues.

What becomes clear through an in-depth exploration of Black political thought is that conservatism is not foreign or

imposed but rather has been self-selected by individuals within the Black community based on their evaluation of how best to achieve their goals for themselves, their families, and their communities. Often, this choice is driven by strategies that align with conservative ideologies, such as a healthy respect for law and order, educational choice, and fiscal conservatism.

Society must be honest about the complex political landscape, embracing it rather than shying away from its intricacies. **Just as with any other group of people, the Black community represents a multitude of ideological perspectives that must be acknowledged to foster a true democratic discourse**. It is through such recognition and understanding that we inch closer to realizing a more comprehensive appreciation for the vast expanse of American political ideology.

When engaging readers in this topic, a conversational tone must be adopted, one that reflects the authority of a teacher yet invites dialogue. It is not a lecture to be delivered; rather, **it's a shared exploration of ideas, prompting readers to question respectfully and seek deeper understanding**. It is in this exchange, rooted in humility and curiosity, that misconceptions can be dismantled, and growth can be fostered.

While it is crucial to teach and clarify, it is equally important to illustrate through storytelling. Vignettes of Black conservatives, from local community leaders to towering national figures, enliven the text with logical proof points and trigger shared emotional sentiments within the reader. Sharing these narratives can transform abstract concepts into tangible experiences, bridging the gap between theory and reality.

Remaining accessible in language and tone does not diminish the quality of the argument but rather amplifies its reach. The facts, when presented plainly and confidently, have their own resonance; they speak to a truth that doesn't require embellishment. Herein lies the persuasive force of the narrative — its ability to unveil complex truths in a manner that is intuitive and compelling.

Historical Foundations of Conservative Principles

Throughout our quest for understanding, historical context is paramount. To comprehend the present, we must acknowledge the contours of the past; conservative principles did not surface in the Black community as an anomaly but stemmed from a robust lineage of self-determination and moral values. Recognizing this heritage dismantles stereotypes and offers a clearer vision of the role Black conservatism plays in shaping American politics.

Demystifying Misconceptions

Our aim is to enlighten and to dispel the shadows cast by long-standing misconceptions. The fabric of Black political thought is diverse, and the threads of conservatism are interwoven into the larger, dynamic pattern. As you read on, you will find stories of innovation, resilience, and faith that underscore the impact of conservative ideologies within the Black community.

Respect for the diversity of thought is the bedrock of democracy, and as such, it remains a guiding principle in the narrative ahead. Whether in political discourse, economic strategies, or social ideals, the voices of Black conservatives deserve a platform unfettered by false presumptions, malicious name-calling, and attempted silencing by "cancel culture".

The Path Forward

As we progress through this book, each chapter aims to empower and encourage. We will explore the pioneering spirits that defy easy categorization and the strategic minds that chart courses for growth and prosperity. Alongside, we will integrate wisdom from varied disciplines, from theological virtues that inspire to economic policies that produce real-world success.

We stand at the threshold of a deeper understanding, an invitation to engage in a collective journey of exploration. The chapters to come promise to embolden readers, drawing from a wellspring of knowledge and real-life examples that equip us to navigate the multifaceted landscape of Black conservatism.

Our conversation here is one of revelation and respect, forging connections and igniting a sense of shared purpose. Together, we navigate the full spectrum of political beliefs, strategies for prosperity, and the deeply-held values that unite us.

And so, our journey continues with an understanding that our diversity of thought is not just a strength, but a testament to the complexity and resilience inherent in the American spirit. We go forward with a call to action: be curious, stay informed, and embrace the untold spectrum of conservatism as a vital component of our nation's ongoing narrative.

Chapter Two

The Crossroads of Liberty: Government in the Eyes of Black Conservatism

A mid the bustling cafe, the clink of coffee cups and the murmur of earnest conversation provided a mosaic of urban life. Marcus, sitting at a corner table, his laptop open but idle, was far removed from the caffeine-infused productivity around him. In his mind, the words of Frederick Douglass whispered alongside the prose of Booker T. Washington, painting a portrait of his current conundrum.

Marcus was a businessman, a community leader, and by many measures, a guiding light in his neighborhood. He believed strongly in personal responsibility and entrepreneurship, values instilled in him from his upbringing, which resonated with the tenets of Black conservative thought he had heard articulated by contemporary voices like Thomas Sowell. Yet, today, his faith was guiding him towards a new challenge.

There were murmurs in the community about the lack of opportunity and the regulatory roadblocks established by what some saw as an overbearing government presence. He pondered upon the words of Proverbs 15:22, *"Without counsel, plans go awry, but in the multitude of counselors they are established."* Marcus knew the importance of the community coming together for counsel, to bridge the historic perspective on government's role between Black conservatives and liberals to find common ground.

Marcus saw entrepreneurship as an act of faith, a trust in the talents God bestowed upon each individual to cultivate and grow. He yearned to create opportunities for his community members to experience this form of empowerment and self-reliance. Yet, he was acutely aware of the contemporary policy approaches that distinguished Black conservative ideology, pressing for minimal government intervention, which often contradicted the liberal emphasis on expansive social programs provided by the government.

He recalled a town hall meeting, where fiery debates seemed an impassioned symphony: lyrics of government assistance clashing with the melody of governmental restraint. The promise of American freedom, juxtaposed with the heavy chains of generational disenfranchisement, underscored the need for balance and wisdom to navigate these tumultuous waters.

As he returned to the present, Marcus took a sip of his now lukewarm coffee, grounding himself with its bitter taste, reflecting how similarly, life presented moments both bitter and sweet. It was then that a young woman approached him, her eyes alight with the spark of ambition, seeking mentorship on starting her own business.

"The Lord gives strength to his people; the Lord blesses his people with peace," he muttered under his breath, as he closed his laptop to give her his full attention. As they embarked on a dialogue about business plans and community engagement, Marcus recognized this as the manifestation of his thoughts into actions — entrepreneurial mentorship as a pillar of faith.

With the sun setting, casting shadows through the cafe windows, which seemed to reach out and embrace the young woman's dreams, Marcus felt a burgeoning sense of purpose, guided by his faith and his conservative principles. He pondered if his efforts to reconcile these distinct ideologies could bear fruit in his community.

Could this young woman's journey mark the beginning of a renewed era where personal accountability, entrepreneurship, and the utilization of conservative policy approaches empower and unite a community otherwise divided?

At the Intersection of Principle and Polity

Within these pages lies a dissection of how historic differences in perspective have shaped—and continue to shape—the Black conservative's view on governance. **This is not simply a matter of political loyalty; it is a reflection of deeply held beliefs** about the nature of freedom, the imperative of personal responsibility, and the transformative power of enterprise.

Exploring the historic schism between conservative and liberal ideologies among Black Americans begins with understanding the bedrock of Black conservatism: a profound respect for the principles of liberty and self-governance as espoused by

the founders of the United States. The discourse often unravels along the lines of historical context and perceived roles that different governments have played in the lives of Black communities. **For Black conservatives, the government's role is construed as a platform to uplift through enabling legislation, rather than to provide continuous aid that people depend on indefinitely.** This preference for smaller government intervention is contrasted by liberal counterparts who often advocate for more significant government roles in equalizing opportunities and outcomes.

In elucidating the crucial role of personal accountability and entrepreneurship, this ideology draws inspiration from the spiritual ideal of stewardship. There is a belief that each individual is blessed with talents and opportunities that must be cultivated with diligence and foresight. **For many Black conservatives, achievement is not merely a personal triumph but is viewed as a divine mandate to utilize one's God-given potential fully.** Recognizing the socioeconomic disparities, Black conservatism advocates for economic empowerment through business ownership and job creation, thereby venerating the virtues of hard work and self-reliance.

In the modern political arena, distinct policy approaches define Black conservative thought. This leans heavily on market-based solutions to socio-economic problems, a stance that can appear at odds with more collective-oriented strategies favored by progressives. Nowhere is this more palpable than **in matters of education reform, where school choice and parental control stand as pillars against one-size-fits-all public education systems.** Similarly, tax policy and regulatory reform are espoused as means to foster a climate where businesses, especially in underserved communities, can thrive to build generational wealth and to revitalize communities.

Across the echelons of society, Black conservative leaders underscore the potency of role modeling and mentorship. They not only preach but also practice the gospel of lifting others by creating opportunities within their own circles of influence. These real-world examples permeate the narrative, providing a canvas to illustrate how Black conservatism operates in practice, beyond academic theorization or political rhetoric.

In the grand analysis, this exploration transcends a mere comparison of Black conservative and liberal thought; it is a narrative about American ideals seen through a particular lens. The hope here is to illuminate the role of foundational spiritual and economic principles in crafting an ideology that champions liberty, self-sufficiency, and communal prosperity. The mantle of Black conservatism may be complex and at times contentious; yet, it is undeniably rich with teachings of resilience, ambition, and faith-driven determination.

Understanding the varying approaches to the role of government holds the key to deciphering the profound chasm between Black conservatives and liberals throughout American history. For Black conservatives, there's been a persistent belief in self-sufficiency and limited government intervention. **The government is not their savior.** This conviction has roots deeply embedded in the principles of spiritual dignity and independence. It is drawn from the biblical notion that the empowerment and welfare of the individual and the community stem from self-reliant endeavors, with the book of 2 Thessalonians echoing that "if anyone is not willing to work, let him not eat." (2 Thessalonians 3:10)

Black liberal ideology, conversely, has traditionally emphasized the government's responsibility to rectify social injustices and dismantle systemic barriers. This perspective is often associated with the prophetic call for social justice outlined in scriptures like the book of Psalms, imploring readers to *"defend the weak and the fatherless; uphold the cause of the poor and the oppressed"* (Psalm 82:3), an invocation for compassionate governance to aid those marginalized. **This is a good example of how divergent viewpoints draw upon a shared spiritual heritage but interpret the text to support markedly different roles for government.**

In the crucible of slavery and the decades that followed, many Black leaders like Booker T. Washington espoused the virtues of industry and entrepreneurial spirit. They believed African Americans could best achieve equality through economic success and personal accountability, a philosophy that laid the bedrock for Black conservatism. Washington's narrative didn't discount the role of the government; however, it underlined a type of partnership where the state supported, rather than led, the community's efforts to prosper.

Moving through the Civil Rights era, a generational shift began to evolve. Many African Americans, empowered by newly secured rights, still found themselves facing the residual effects of slavery and segregation. Black liberalism argued for the state's active hand in creating conditions for equality, supporting legislation like affirmative action and an overarching welfare state. These policies were intended as a corrective force, a means by which society would acknowledge systemic disparities and foster a more fair societal landscape.

Yet, throughout this monumental period, figures like Thomas Sowell and later, Clarence Thomas, championed the importance of meritocracy and individual endeavor. Their conservative viewpoints insisted that reliance on government intervention could potentially stunt the community's growth by fostering dependency rather than self-reliance and that long-term success was rooted in education and hard work over assistive legislation.

Today, Black conservatism continues to explore the balance between individual initiative and the government's role in public life, maintaining that **less regulation and lower taxes can spur innovation and wealth creation, benefitting African Americans and the broader society alike.** The emphasis lies prominently on creating economic policies that encourage small business development and private sector solutions to address what they perceive as the incapacitating effects of overbearing governmental influence.

Guiding Principles or Government Handouts: Navigating the Current Landscape

The Principle of Personal Accountability

At the core of Black conservative thought lies the unwavering principle of personal accountability. **This belief is rooted in the notion that one's success or failure is, by and large, a result of individual effort and decision-making.** It's a perspective that aligns closely with many proverbs and teachings found within spiritual texts, which consistently advocate for personal responsibility as a pathway to fulfillment. **This bedrock of accountability upholds the conviction that by taking ownership of one's actions and their consequences, individuals not only develop a resilient character but also foster a strong community wherein each member thrives through mutual respect and self-discipline.**

Entrepreneurship as a Vehicle for Empowerment

Entrepreneurship holds a significant place within Black conservative ideals, viewed not just as a means to economic prosperity but as a manifestation of liberty and self-determination. **For many, the entrepreneurial journey represents the penultimate exercise of freedom — the ability to create, build, and sustain according to one's vision.** As a mentor would advise a protégé, black conservatism encourages the pursuit of entrepreneurial goals with a combination of faith, hard work, and unyielding perseverance. It is believed that through these endeavors, not only do individuals empower themselves, but they also contribute to the economic stability and growth of their communities.

Linking Tenacity to Tradition

Drawing upon the rich history of innovation and enterprise within the Black community, Black conservatives often look to past trailblazers as exemplars of independent spirit. Stories of individuals who overcame adversity through their own ingenuity and resilience act as testimonials to the transformative power of personal accountability. These narratives, paired with time-honored wisdom, are utilized to inspire action and underline the tenet that one's destiny can be shaped by tenacity and self-reliance, even in the face of systemic challenges.

Nurturing an Economically Minded Mindset

Within Black conservatism, much emphasis is placed on economic literacy as a cornerstone of empowerment. Fundamental understandings of wealth creation, investment, and fiscal management are championed, driven by the principle that financial independence is a precursor to broader freedoms. By integrating perspectives from economics with life lessons, Black conservative thinkers strive to equip their communities with actionable strategies to navigate and succeed in the free market economy. It is in this vein that financial literacy is not merely about personal gain — it is seen as an act of self-empowerment that enriches both the individual and the wider society.

Sowing Seeds of Success Through Mentorship

Mentorship holds a treasured role in perpetuating the values of Black conservatism. Experience teaches that wisdom gleaned from seasoned entrepreneurs and professionals can light the path for emerging leaders. Thus, successful figures within the community often prioritize the nurturing of young talent, imparting guidance and facilitating opportunities for the next generation. This nurturing is a tangible demonstration of the communal orientation inherent in Black conservative thought, where **success is most meaningful when shared and multiplied across the collective**.

Crafting Policy with Principle

When the conversation turns to policy, Black conservatives advocate for initiatives that reinforce self-sufficiency and limit dependency on government intervention. **The legislative approaches backed by Black conservative ideology are typically those that create the conditions for personal endeavors to flourish** — through tax reforms, deregulation, and educational choice, for example. These policy preferences are undergirded by the conviction that with the right framework, individuals - not the government - are fully capable of crafting their destinies and elevating their communities.

Upholding Faith in the Public Sphere

An aspect not to be overlooked is the significant role of faith in Black conservative ideology. While personal accountability and entrepreneurship are esteemed, they are often contextually enveloped by a spiritual ethos that regards material success as one component of a broader, purpose-driven life. The integration of faith into public life and policy is advocated not as an imposition of religious doctrine, but as a way to support religious liberty and to infuse society with spiritually-linked values of integrity, compassion, and stewardship.

Laying the Foundations of Black Conservative Thought

Historical Context

The maturation of Black conservative ideology can be traced back to the crucible of the Civil Rights Era. It has burgeoned into a potent force in contemporary political discourse, but its roots are deep and historic. Historical context serves to illustrate the timeline of the movement, pinpointing pivotal moments where Black conservatism diverged from its liberal counterpart. Recognizing figures like Booker T. Washington and the U.S. Senator Tim Scott, this facet underscores the contribution of Black conservative voices advocating for self-help, skill development and economic independence as tools for racial advancement and inclusion.

Ideological Foundations

Black conservatism is moored to a set of ideological foundations that emphasize **limited government intervention, free-market principles, individual liberty, and personal accountability**. These cornerstones diverge from mainstream conservatism through their nuanced understanding of racial dynamics in America. **Black conservative thought champions the power of the individual while remaining cognizant of the complex social histories shaping Black American experiences**. It is this balance of reverence for traditional conservative values with a strong, sometimes critical, engagement with the legacy of race that differentiates the philosophy and fortifies its relevance.

Socioeconomic Factors

Within the Black conservative movement, there is a keen awareness of the ways in which socioeconomic factors shape political leanings. Issues such as economic disenfranchisement and the debate over welfare and affirmative action policies have forged a distinct set of priorities. **Advocates argue that too much governmental dependency can stifle personal initiative and undermine the family structure, proposing instead policies favoring economic empowerment and supporting entrepreneurship**. This pillar of the framework scrutinizes the conduits through which socioeconomic realities inform and propel the advocacy for conservative approaches to social welfare and economic growth.

Political Influences

The political sway exerted on the Black Conservative Movement has ebbed and flowed with the changing tides of American politics. Central to this model is the examination of electoral dynamics, the realignment within political parties, and the impact of policy advocacy. This sector acknowledges the sway of influential Black conservatives who, through elective office, activism, or analytical punditry, have carved pathways for the movement's ideas to permeate the political landscape. It scrutinizes how key party platforms and national debates have either constrained or catalyzed the progress of Black conservatism.

Cultural Elements

At its core, Black conservatism intrinsically connects with cultural pillars, influenced by the rich tapestry of African American traditions and the significant impact of faith on social values. It recognizes the role of intellectuals and artists in **articulating a vision for Black America that is both culturally authentic and ideologically conservative**. This strand of the framework considers how the interplay between cultural identity and political ideology has crafted a unique narrative within the Black conservative movement, promoting principles that resonate with wider segments of the Black community.

Synergy and Interaction

Upon examining the individual components above, it becomes clear that their interplay is integral to understanding the comprehensive picture of Black conservative thought. Historical legacies inform the ideological positioning which, together with socioeconomic and political elements, coalesce within a cultural context to shape a dynamic conservative ideology. Each factor is not isolated but interde-

pendent, creating a network of influence that adapts and evolves with
the passage of time and shifting societal conditions.

As we reflect upon the varied perspectives on government's role in
society, it becomes evident that **Black conservatism upholds the
fundamental principle that government should serve as a fa-
cilitator, not an inhibitor, of individual liberty and prosperity.** In the Scriptures, it is often taught that every individual bears
responsibility for their actions, a principle that resonates with the
Black conservative viewpoint. Proverbs 14:23 affirms, *"All hard work
brings a profit, but mere talk leads only to poverty."* Drawing from this
wisdom, Black conservatives emphasize personal accountability and
the entrepreneurial spirit as the engines of success.

Personal accountability is not just a concept, but a clarion call to
action, urging individuals to take ownership of their own destinies.
The stories of prominent black entrepreneurs who have transformed
their lives through hard work and perseverance are both instructive
and illustrative of this tenet's profound impact. They remind us that
our path to achievement, both spiritual and material, is paved with
intention and discipline. Let their successes be a beacon, motivating
us to rise and chase our own visions with unwavering determination.

Entrepreneurship, accordingly, stands as a revered pillar within this
ideological framework. It is seen as a pathway to economic salvation
and self-reliance, a fulfillment of the biblical charge in Ecclesiastes
9:10: *"Whatever your hand finds to do, do it with all your might."* In
this light, the pursuit of business and economic growth is not merely
a financial endeavor — it's a moral imperative that reverberates with
spiritual significance. As individuals seek success, they embody the
true spirit of freedom that Black conservatism cherishes.

When examining contemporary policy approaches, Black conservatives often diverge markedly from their liberal counterparts. They

advocate for policies that prioritize economic freedom and limited government intervention. Solutions that empower communities through education, access to capital, and the removal of bureaucratic obstacles are favored over expansive government programs. **This focus on self-sufficiency aligns closely with a belief in the providence of opportunity for all who are willing to work earnestly for it** — a concept central to the American Dream.

Empowerment Through Action

In grasping these principles, we must move beyond mere contemplation and into the realm of action. It is our responsibility to cultivate environments where freedom and entrepreneurship can flourish. This is not an abstract mission but a tangible endeavor. Promoting policies that protect economic freedom, supporting businesses that create opportunities within communities, and advocating for education that prepares the next generation for success are all concrete strategies that reflect Black conservative ideals.

Moreover, we must remain vigilant in safeguarding the liberties that enable us to live and work in accordance with our deepest convictions. The value of this vigilance cannot be overstated, for it is through the preservation of liberty that we ensure the continuity of a society where each person can actualize their potential, unencumbered by the undue constraints of an overreaching government.

The Charge for the Future

As stewards of our shared future, we bear the responsibility to inspire, guide, and uplift those who look to us for direction. The knowledge we impart and the actions we take will ripple through time, impacting generations to come. May our efforts be guided by wisdom, our hearts by compassion, and our initiatives by the indomitable spirit that defines the enduring legacy of Black conservatism. Let us commit to being agents of change, champions of liberty, and exemplars of the prosperity that arises from a life led with diligence and faith.

Chapter Three

Party Lines: The Tumultuous Dance with Democrats and Republicans

S unset in Savannah had always been a subdued affair, painting the sky with strokes of tangerine and lilac, softening the edges of the day into the calm of evening. James stood outside the town hall, the aged bricks a muted witness to his inner turmoil. The air was heavy with the fragrance of magnolias drifting from the nearby square, meshing with his contemplative mood. His gaze, reflecting a tumultuous history, looked past the iron-wrought fences to a gathering of his community members, their conversations humming like a hive intent on thriving amidst adversity.

He was an anomaly; a Black conservative grappling with the ghosts of the Republican Party's past alliances, his soul weighted by the complex tapestry of the civil rights struggle that had painted vast swathes of his people with a Democrat blue. The echoes of spiritual teachings hummed in his mind, a steady rhythm of justice and equality that had always underscored his political choices, yet now left him questioning the path laid before him. Could faith reconcile with a political doctrine that seemed so misaligned with the community he so dearly cherished?

Inside the town hall, James prepared to address his supporters. He carried not only the burden of historical precedence but also the aspiration to redefine what it meant to be a Black conservative in today's fractured political landscape. He outlined his vision with the certainty of a man who had dined at the table of wisdom, quoting Proverbs 29:7, *"The righteous care about justice for the poor, but the wicked have no such concern."* He spoke not only to those present but reached out to touch the hearts of a wider congregation, yearning to awaken a sense of pragmatism within their ideological leanings.

James paced the stage with measured confidence, offering a roadmap towards economic empowerment, an entrepreneurial spirit as his compass. Like Nehemiah rebuilding the walls of Jerusalem, James urged his listeners to construct their futures with diligence and unity. He parlayed his expertise into motivational charge, his stance clear and resolute against the headwinds of opposition that often felt like the spray of the Atlantic during a churning storm.

Under the guidance of his mentors, James had learned to weave insights as diverse as the colors in Joseph's coat – vivid narratives of empowerment entwined with threads of conservatism, drawing strength from biblical teachings, political studies, and economic principles alike. He invited his audience into a conversation, a gentle but firm summons to explore the deep waters where faith and policy, skin color and political affiliation, intersected and often clashed.

As James concluded his speech, the promises of change resonated with the weight of historical significance and current relevance. His voice, warm yet filled with steely resolve, implored not for unified agreement but for respectful engagement and understanding, beckoning his listeners to consider their legacy and the future they wished to mold. The air, now cooler as the heat of the day ebbed, seemed to carry away the remnants of division, leaving behind a potent mix of anticipation and introspection. And so, with night descending upon Savannah, a question lingered, begging for reflection: Are we, as a people, bound by the shackles of history and selective memory, or can we forge new chains of understanding, linking past wisdom with modern convictions?

Navigating the Tightrope of Bipartisan Allegiance

Black conservatism has long threaded the delicate line between steadfast patriotism and the fierce advocacy for the civil rights that underpin the American ethos. It is within this complex interplay that **Black conservatives have crafted a political identity that often bucks conventional party boundaries**. The tumultuous dance with Democrats and Republicans reveals a rich tapestry woven by Black political pioneers who have both shaped and been shaped by the nation's party lines. This historical narrative is not simply one of shifting allegiances but a profound quest for political representation that aligns with core values and the relentless pursuit of justice and equality.

The relationship between Black conservatives and the Republican Party is intrinsically tied to both historical context and evolving ideologies. **As the GOP once stood as the party of Lincoln and the abolition crusade, it attracted the early allegiance of Black voters**. However, historical winds shifted over time leading into the civil rights movement and the subsequent realignment of party platforms. The complexities of this transition aren't merely a footnote in history; they exemplify the principled navigation required to remain true to both conservative values and a commitment to civil rights. The examination of this evolution not only underscores political realignment but also serves as a testament to the adaptability and resilience within the Black conservative ethos.

In the wake of the civil rights era, the seismic shift of Black voter allegiance to the Democratic Party created an intriguing dynamic for Black conservatives. Faced with an evolving political landscape, they began to reassess how to interact with and within the mainstream conservative movement. This reevaluation uncovered challenges and opportunities alike, as it prompted a deeper introspection regarding party affiliation and policy advocacy. Herein lies the challenge: maintaining an allegiance to conservatism while confronting the perceived monolithic voting trends of Black Americans.

Today's political terrain for Black conservatives is as convoluted as it is charged with potential. With the two-party system presenting stark contrasts, Black conservatives often find themselves in a dance of diplomacy, advocating for policies that sometimes transcend traditional party platforms. Within this intricate political labyrinth, they represent a diverse spectrum of thought, challenging the binary political narrative and inciting new conversations on what it truly means to be a conservative of color in America.

Patriotic Prudence: Evaluating Political Candidates with Integrity

The heart of democracy thrives on informed and active participation. Here is a meticulous process that allows one to proceed with both wisdom and insight:

1. **Values and Visions**: Begin by reflecting on your convictions. It is critical to comprehend the issues that resonate deeply with your beliefs and the collective well-being of your community. Ranging from healthcare to social issues, these key topics will guide your discerning eye when examining prospective leaders.

2. **Harvest of Information**: Immerse yourself in the backgrounds of political aspirants. Scrutinize their campaign manifestos, delve into their past legislative endeavors, and angle for their stances on the issues you hold dear. This methodical gathering is foundational to an insightful evaluation.

3. **Markers of Trust**: Evaluate the integrity and credibility of each candidate. A consistent track record, untarnished by scandals and rooted in a transparent approach to finance, speaks volumes about their reliability as potential officeholders.

4. **Alliance Assessment**: Consider who backs each candidate. Endorsements reflect mutual philosophies and can influence policy — ensure these affiliations resonate with your principles.

5. **Capability Analysis**: Leadership is both an art and a science. Examine the aptitude of the candidates—do they harbor the skills to lead, collaborate, and inspire? Genuine competence is an irreplaceable asset in governance.

6. **Direct Discourse**: Whenever possible, engage directly with political campaigns. Town halls and debates are fertile grounds to gauge sincerity and understand the personas behind the platforms.

7. **Diverse Discernment**: Seek a breadth of perspectives. Inundate yourself with various credible sources, for the truth often lies at the intersection of disparate viewpoints.

8. **Electability Estimate**: Evaluate the pragmatics of potential success. While idealism is commendable, the practicalities of victory are not to be overlooked, as they hold sway over the feasibility of enacting desired policies.

9. **Reflect and Resolve**: Synthesize your research into a decision. Weigh the pros and cons, align them closely with your values, and prioritize accordingly.

10. **Active Advocacy**: Translate your decision into action. Contribute to the campaign of your choice through volunteering, financial support, or by advocating within your circles, for it is through direct action that civic engagement finds its most potent expression.

This endeavor is a manifestation of responsibility that beckons every voting citizen. It is through such thoughtful engagement with the electoral process that the ideal of a truly representative democracy may inch closer to fruition.

The relationship between Black conservatives and the Republican Party has a lineage deeply woven into the very fabric of American history. **The Republican Party, known as the party of Lincoln, advocated for the abolition of slavery and was widely supported by African Americans post-Civil War.** This historical backdrop is essential in understanding the foundations of allegiance which laid the groundwork for Black conservatism within the party.

African American conservatives found, in the Republican Party's values of individualism, self-reliance, and limited government, a resonating echo of the spiritual principles that had long fortified their communities against adversity. They gravitated toward policies that they felt would foster economic independence and moral responsibility, drawing on Biblical teachings that underscore the virtues of hard work and personal accountability.

The ideological kinship that Black conservatives had with the Republican Party was not merely a political convenience, but rather a deep-seated alignment of values and vision for America. Figures like **Booker T. Washington became emblematic of Black conservatism in this era, championing economic self-sufficiency and incremental gains over more radical shifts in the social order. Washington's famous *Atlanta Compromise* speech elucidated the strategic patience and self-improvement ethos that came to characterize a segment of African American political thought.** To this day, it remains a testament to the political pragmatism that informed Black conservative engagement with the Republican Party.

Nevertheless, the fidelity to the Republican Party witnessed among Black conservatives was not without its challenges and nuances. As the 20th century progressed, the party began to undergo significant ideological shifts. **The New Deal policies of Franklin D. Roosevelt attracted many African Americans to the Democratic Party, and the Republican Party's stance on civil rights became an increasingly fraught issue**. Despite these changes, a contingent of Black conservatives sustained their allegiance, guided by a belief in the meritocratic ideals and economic principles of conservatism.

By the mid-20th century, the Civil Rights Movement and the Republican Party's embrace of the Southern Strategy further complicated the political landscape for Black conservatives. While the majority of African Americans shifted their loyalty to the Democrats, who were now championing civil rights, some Black conservatives continued to advocate for policy over party, seeking to reform the Republican Party from within. They argued that economic empowerment was inseparable from civil rights and that the Republican principles of free enterprise and small government could be harnessed to achieve racial equality.

The emergence of neoconservatism in the latter part of the century provided new rhetorical and intellectual foundations that attracted Black conservatives. The emphasis on law and order, skepticism towards welfare programs, and a hardline stance against Communism resonated with those who saw economic liberalism and strong family values as the keys to progress.

Moving toward actionable insights, one must consider how Black conservative entrepreneurs and business leaders have worked to align economic initiatives with the broader goals of the community. Individuals like Robert L. Johnson, founder of Black Entertainment Television, employed market-based strategies to create wealth and opportunities within African American communities, reinforcing the potential of a conservative business model aligned with communal growth.

The historical relationship between Black conservatives and the Republican Party is a narrative replete with ideological commitments and strategic alignments. It underscores the vibrant complexity of Black political identity, disabusing simplistic notions of monolithic voting behavior. As we move forward into the present day, it is imperative to bear in mind how these deep-rooted affiliations have morphed, confronted new realities, and posed fresh questions for African American conservatives.

Navigating Political Allegiances: A Modern Challenge

The Post-Civil Rights Realignment of Black Voters

The civil rights era was a seismic shift in American politics, dramatically altering the political landscape, particularly for Black Americans. Before the 1960s, Black Americans had a history of Republican alignment, largely due to the party's roots with Abraham Lincoln and the Emancipation Proclamation. However, the Democratic Party's support for civil rights legislation during the 1960s catalyzed a mass migration of Black voters to the Democratic fold. This transition represented not just a change in party preference but a fundamental reshaping of political identities. **For Black conservatives, it posed a challenging paradox as their traditional values seemed increasingly at odds with the Republican Party's evolving platform, which by the 1980s, often appeared indifferent or even hostile to civil rights concerns.**

The Impact on Black Conservatives

For Black conservatives, the realignment meant navigating twin cur-
rents of ideological allegiance and racial justice. They found themselves in a delicate balance, advocating for fiscal conservatism and personal responsibility, while also confronting the enduring realities of
racial inequality. The Republican Party's shift towards a more conservative stance on social issues coupled with strategies, like the Southern
Strategy, which many interpreted to be racially insensitive, left many
Black conservatives struggling to reconcile their conservative philosophy with a party they felt was alienating them and their communities.
**The challenge was to maintain their convictions while fighting
against the perception of being outliers within their own racial
cohort and within the party they traditionally supported.**

The political landscape for Black conservatives today is as dynamic
as it has ever been. The two-party system in the United States often
delineates a binary option for voters, yet **many Black conservative
voices resist simplistic categorization, feeling tension pulling
them from both the left and the right. These individuals, myself
included, may find their values resonate with certain Republican ideals, such as emphasis on family, faith, and individual
autonomy. However, they must also navigate a complex social
terrain where the GOP's recent outreach to ethnic minorities
has been questionably effective, and where enduring loyalties to
the Democratic Party continue to influence familial and community ties.**

Navigating this landscape requires a nuanced understanding of
identity and policy. **Many Black conservatives express a frustration with being seen as outliers within their communities and**

/ **or as anomalies within their chosen political party**. Such experiences call for a deeper conversation around political affiliation that transcends the color lines often drawn by society. This conversation aligns well with spiritual principles that advocate for unity and the importance of the individual soul over superficial differences, similar to Galatians 3:28.

Moreover, the charge often leveled against the Black conservative — that of betraying one's racial identity in favor of a political one — is a gross oversimplification. Engaging in thoughtful discourse and respectful debate around policy and party affiliation is a testament to the intellectual diversity within the Black community. It honors the rich history of Black thought leaders who have grappled with varied ideologies to craft strategies for empowerment and liberation. **Let's eradicate the stereotype that "all black people must think alike".**

In the current climate, Black conservatives are becoming increasingly more visible, challenging the narrative that Blackness and conservatism are fundamentally at odds. For me, growing up to see former Secretary of State Colin Powell and former Secretary of State Condoleezza Rice highlights the presence of Black individuals in high-profile conservative roles in modern times. Yet it's not just in the echelons of power where this redefinition is taking place; it's occurring in communities and at the grassroots level, where voices are challenging the traditional party lines and advocating for what they believe will forge a better future.

The Legacy of Black Conservatism and the Republican Party

As we recount the historical relationship between Black conservatives and the Republican Party, we are reminded of a robust connection shaped by shared values and mutual aspirations for progress. The Republican Party, once a beacon for the civil rights of African Americans, has often presented itself as the party of Lincoln, emphasizing emancipation and equal rights. This storied past has been marked by both synergy and tension, as Black conservatives have had to navigate their own community's shifting allegiances and the evolving ideologies of the party itself. Reflecting on this journey leads to an important recognition: **that political affiliations are not immutable, and that they should be guided by principle rather than party. For those Black conservatives who have felt alienated in the political sphere, there is a clarion call to perseverance and informed action.**

Today's Political Landscape and Beyond

As we turn our gaze to the current political landscape, we recognize that Black conservatives continue to confront a complex matrix of challenges and opportunities. The two-party system, though often polarizing, can also be a platform for nuanced dialogue and substantive proposals. **The informed Black conservative knows that deep understanding and clear-sighted strategies pave the way to meaningful influence, both within the political parties and in broader society.**

In the sphere of modern politics, the collective experience and wisdom of those who have navigated these tumultuous waters before becomes invaluable. Personal anecdotes and real-world examples of Black conservatives who have reached across party lines to effect change underscore the practical ways in which individuals can make a difference. They act as instructive signposts for how to engage constructively and with conviction, regardless of the prevailing political winds.

Empowerment stems from a steadfast commitment to one's principles and the courage to voice them, even in the face of opposition. It is this spirit that must animate the path forward for Black conservatives, encouraging them to leverage their unique perspectives in shaping a more inclusive and prosperous future. In doing so, they are charged with the noble task of defining the contours of the movement for generations to come, **ensuring that the diversity of thought remains a hallmark of American conservatism.**

Fundamentally, the dance with Democrats and Republicans is less about loyalty to a party and more about aligning policy with timeless values and the pursuit of common good. As Black conservatives look ahead, they must continue to be stewards of a legacy that transcends party lines — a legacy built on the bedrock of faith, resilience, and an unwavering commitment to the dream of a more perfect union.

In fostering an environment that values robust discourse, mutual respect, and a shared vision for the future, the contributions of Black conservatives can and should be a unifying thread. Their voices, seasoned by the past and attuned to the present, carry the promise of a profound and transformative influence on the political landscape. Addressing social inequities, championing fiscal responsibility, and advocating for traditional values, they reflect a rich and multifaceted ideology — one that inherently recognizes that America's strength lies in its ability to honor and synthesize a plethora of voices and experiences.

By embracing this dual role of tradition-bearer and innovator, Black conservatives step into a space of great potential and responsibility. It is within this space—where conviction meets challenge and diversity of thought is celebrated—that strategies are formed, alliances are built, and the possibilities for progress are boundless. With determination and clear vision, they will continue to write the next chapters of this dynamic and evolving story—one that, undoubtedly, holds significance far beyond the confines of a single chapter or book.

Chapter Four

Against the Grain: Black Conservatives Challenging Policy Prescriptions

I n the corner of an old library, heavy with the scent of aged paper and whispering with the quiet echo of intellectual pursuit, Michael sat with a book sprawled open in his hands. The afternoon sun sliced through the windows, casting bars of light across his dark skin and the worn pages before him. On these pages were words, debates, and viewpoints that were slowly constructing a scaffold for his worldviews.

He pondered the notions of fiscal responsibility, as posited by the authors identifying as Black conservatives. A gentle breeze moved the pages forward, as though challenging him to look beyond traditional thinking. Michael recalled his uncle, a stern figure whose commanding respect stemmed from the success he attained through sheer perseverance. His uncle preached that personal accountability and wise financial stewardship were the bedrock of prosperity. Michael's inner dialogue ran over these values, contrasting them with the seemingly perennial struggles of his community.

His reflection was interrupted by a soft enquiry from an old library attendant, offering guidance. Michael declined with a polite nod and returned to the solitude of his thoughts, diving next into the contentious issue of affirmative action. The book before him critiqued such policies with a conservative lens, suggesting that merit should triumph over mandatory diversity quotas. As he read, his mind wandered to his sister, a bright spark who had recently embarked on her college journey, her path smoothed by such policies. Was it truly unfair, he wondered, or was it a necessary redress?

He could almost hear his father's voice, rich with the timber of conviction, arguing that the traditional nuclear family structures were essential for nurturing discipline, patriotism and Judeo-Christian values. It was within this crucible that free-market capitalism was vindicated, for, in such families, as his father believed, the spirit of entrepreneurship and self-reliance flourished. Michael felt this principle deeply, as steel beams in the skyscrapers his forebears had built, standing tall and resolute against the tests of time and economy.

His fingers traced the lineage of thoughts and tales in the book, connecting dots that spanned theology, politics, and the gritty realities of business. Stories of Black entrepreneurs who built empires from their humble beginnings filled him with an intangible warmth, a burning spark of aspiration. Amid these historic and modern-day proverbs, he recognized the persuasive tapestry of hard work and divine grace woven together by his ancestors' hands.

The day aged and shadows began to sprawl across the room, like the extended branches of a great oak. Michael felt rooted, yet ready to rise. As the final sliver of sunlight vanished, leaving only the soft amber glow of the library lamps, the conviction for his path seemed clearer.

Could Michael blend the tenets of Black conservatism with his own compass, to help architect a more equitable, empowered future for his community? What role would his faith play in reconciling these ideals with the diverse tapestry of modern society?

Challenging the Status Quo with Principled Conviction

The narrative of Black conservatism often sits like a dissonant chord in the symphony of American politics, yet it is within this very dissonance that the discourse finds its most profound truth. **Black conservatives offer a perspective that is frequently overlooked: a vision merging fiscal discipline, a critique of well-intentioned but, in their view, misguided policies, and the upholding of traditional values.** The examination of these alternative views is not merely an academic exercise but a call to action and perseverance, firmly rooted in both spiritual principles and pragmatism.

At the heart of Black conservative fiscal beliefs is a commitment to economic empowerment and self-reliance. Scripture tells us that a good steward must be prudent in managing their resources, a principle that Black conservatives extend to government fiscal policy. This chapter seeks to illuminate such principles in addressing national debates on spending and welfare reform. It **reinforces the notion that stewardship and personal responsibility can create a more prosperous society for all citizens, not just black Americans.** As entrepreneurially spirited individuals illustrate, success is frequently borne from the courage to innovate and a relentless pursuit to turn vision into reality.

Speaking out against the grain is a hallmark of Black conservatism when it comes to affirmative action and similar policies. Through a conservative lens, such policies are critiqued for promoting a narrative of dependency rather than empowerment. Citing the common proverb that advocates teaching a man to fish rather than simply providing a fish, Black conservatives argue for policies that promote long-term self-sufficiency rather than short-term assistance. This chapter critically analyzes the impact of these policies and offers alternatives that align with conservative values, ensuring that each individual is judged more by the content of their character, not the color of their skin.

Traditional family structures stand as the bedrock for society — a sentiment that echoes powerfully within Black conservative ideology. **Upholding and revitalizing these nuclear family structures is seen as critical for fostering a strong moral fabric and economic resilience within communities.** With scriptural support, the family unit is sacred and foundational. Without strong families led by strong and faithful fathers, the strength of our churches, neighborhoods, cities, counties, states, and nations are at risk of weakening to the point of complete moral decay. Here, policy implications are debated, highlighting how legislation can either support or erode these pillars of society.

Moreover, there is a spirited endorsement of free-market capitalism, perceived by many Black conservatives as a powerful engine for lifting people out of poverty and providing the canvas upon which personal freedoms are best expressed. This chapter elucidates how the principles of free enterprise not only align with teachings from the scriptures about labor and diligence but also empower individuals to fulfill their potential.

Furthermore, Black conservatives often reference the historical resilience and resourcefulness of Black communities, especially during times when legal and societal barriers were overtly stacked against them. They point to Black Wall Street in Tulsa, Oklahoma—a symbol of Black economic prosperity in the early 20th century—as an example of what could be achieved through community cohesion and financial prudence. Lessons from such histories inform their advocacy for a return to those principles that encourage community investment and discourage over-reliance on external governmental forces.

Government policies, from this perspective, should be catalysts for wealth creation, not crutches that sustain dependence. The advocacy for lower taxes, fewer government regulations, and an emphasis on free-market capitalism is rooted in the conviction that such measures foster an environment where entrepreneurship can flourish. It's in the competitive markets, they argue, where ingenuity is rewarded, job opportunities are created, and financial independence can be secured for all willing to work for it.

Education is also highlighted as a critical avenue for achieving fiscal responsibility. Black conservatives often lament what they see as a lack of emphasis on financial literacy within education systems. By integrating more robust financial education, young people can learn early the value of investing, the power of compound interest, and the dangers of debt — preparing a generation to make informed, prudent financial decisions throughout the rest of their adult lives.

These conservatives do not discredit the role of government entirely but instead offer a reframed vision: Government should empower citizens to be the protagonists in their financial narratives. Borrowing the biblical adage to *"train up a child in the way he should go"* (Proverbs 22:6), the call is for policies that educate and prepare, rather than simply provide. Government programs are therefore encouraged to be structured in ways that incentivize wealth-building and the acquisition of assets.

Navigating the Complex Terrain of Affirmative Action

Affirmative action, though well-intentioned, is a subject of considerable debate, prompting many Black conservatives to voice their concerns about its implications and effectiveness. By advocating for equal opportunity based on merit, they question whether these policies inadvertently stigmatize beneficiaries, implying a necessity for assistance based on racial identity rather than individual merit. **From this perspective, belief in one's inherent capability flourishes when one is evaluated on merit alone** – a principle deeply rooted in faith-based teachings that stress the God-given dignity and potential in every individual. **Such a viewpoint does not ignore historical injustices but strives to ensure that remedies do not foster new forms of dependency or reduction of individual agency.**

Evaluating Outcomes Beyond Intentions

When examining public policies, a conservative lens emphasizes the distinction between intentions and outcomes. While affirmative action aims to rectify past discrimination, its critics argue that the outcomes must be thoroughly assessed. Are these policies creating true equality and empowering individuals, or are they perpetuating a cycle of reliance on external factors for success? Black conservatives often draw upon *proverbs and parables* from spiritual texts that highlight the virtues of self-reliance and personal accountability. Moreover, the tangible results speak volumes; they insist on evaluating the actual advancement within affected communities, supporting policies that empower through upskilling and education, rather than quota systems.

The Meritocracy Principle and Its Economic Implications

From an economic standpoint, Black conservatives argue for the fundamental principles of a meritocracy. In business, results are paramount, and a system that rewards hard work and talent is deemed most effective. Affirmative action, in clouding the clear sight of merit, can be critiqued for potentially insulating organizations from the full competitive pressures of the marketplace. Instead, a focus on nurturing talent and investing in education aligns with the free market's dynamic nature, suggesting that the creation of economic opportunities through fair competition can lead to better outcomes for all demographics.

Upholding Community Values Over Government Intervention

The conservative viewpoint often leans towards community and family structures as foundational elements of support and

development rather than extensive government intervention. Proponents underscore the importance of local community solutions tailored to specific needs, believing these to be more effective and responsive than federal policies like affirmative action. They advocate nurturing values such as hard work, respect, and personal integrity in solving social and economic issues. By doing so, communities can create support systems that bolster individual determination and success, reflecting principles encapsulated in age-old spiritual wisdom that extols the virtues of collective care and personal upliftment.

Forwarding Alternatives to Traditional Affirmative Action

Critics of affirmative action urge the exploration of alternatives that might yield better results. For instance, they argue for more targeted educational programs that bolster competitiveness and resources in disadvantaged communities that equip individuals from an early age. Emphasizing education reform and entrepreneurial mentorship, Black conservatives push for initiatives that empower the youth through knowledge and skill development. Education supported by values of diligence and aspiration can be a powerful equalizer, and coupling this with access to mentors and business leaders provides the practical guidance needed to succeed.

Black Conservatism: A Melting Pot of Five Distinct Perspectives

The Black Conservative Movement encapsulates a rich variety of perspectives, each with its unique characteristics and contributions to the broader conservative tapestry. By examining the model consisting of classical conservatives, libertarian conservatives, religious conservatives, neoconservatives, and pragmatic conservatives, we can gain a clearer understanding of the movement's complexity and the interplay between its components.

Classical Conservatives: Pillars of Tradition and Free Markets

Classical conservatives within the Black community **often advocate for limited government, free-market capitalism, and the preservation of traditional moral values**. They regard fiscal conservatism as key to empowerment and self-reliance, emphasizing the importance of hard work, entrepreneurship, and economic independence. In this framework, **traditional family structures are revered not just as societal cornerstones but as crucibles for fiscal responsibility and moral grounding.** The belief in a smaller government footprint in daily life serves as a bedrock for promoting individual initiative and a robust, competitive economy.

Libertarian Conservatives: Freedom and Personal Responsibility

One step away on the ideological spectrum are libertarian conservatives, who champion **individual liberty and minimal state intervention in personal and economic life**. Their core tenet revolves around the principle that each individual should have the autonomy to choose their path, unimpeded by excessive government regulation. This faction often takes a firm stance on **defending civil liberties and pushing for criminal justice reform** to ensure that the system respects individual rights and corrections focus on rehabilitation and redemption.

Religious Conservatives: Faith and Family at the Forefront

Religious conservatives bring a unique dimension to the conservative mosaic, **deeply intertwining their political beliefs with spiritual convictions**. They emphasize the role of **faith and family values**, often drawing from religious texts to inform their views on social issues ranging from education to the sanctity of life and marriage. **This group advocates for policies that they believe strengthen the family unit and foster a society reflective of their spiritual principles**, asserting that a strong moral fabric underpins a successful and resilient community.

Neoconservatives: Custodians of a Proactive America

Diverging somewhat in terms of foreign policy are the neoconservatives. They merge a commitment to traditional conservative principles with an assertive international stance, underlining the importance of **American exceptionalism** and the nation's duty in shaping global affairs. **Neoconservative black voices typically support a robust national defense and proactive efforts to promote democracy and human rights globally**, seeing this as congruent with the nation's moral and strategic interests.

Pragmatic Conservatives: Steering Towards Achievable Solutions

At the intersection of ideology and practicality are the pragmatic conservatives. They operate on a platform of **seeking effective and feasible solutions** to pressing issues, **prioritizing outcomes over strict adherence to any ideological purity**. Pragmatic conservatives within the Black community might support policies that consider the nuances of racial disparities and seek to bridge gaps through innovation, compromise, and adaptable strategies in areas like healthcare and education.

The synergy between these groups forms a dynamic continuum of thought within Black conservatism, each segment contributing to a robust debate on how best to advance the community's interests while adhering to conservative principles. Many Black conservatives are like myself and see themselves as a hybrid of all five groups of conservatives to varying degrees. While there may be differences in priorities and tactics, these components share a common belief in the power of personal responsibility, the strength derived from faith and family values, and the importance of a society that enables individual freedom within a framework of order and tradition.

The interaction among these factions — classical conservatives inspiring with their vision of a disciplined, economy-focused future; libertarians guarding individual rights; religious voices injecting moral considerations; neoconservatives emphasizing a strong, influential America; and pragmatists seeking bridges where rifts lie — creates a rich dialogue that continuously refines the movement. **As a collective**, these diverse strands assert that conservative values are not only compatible with the Black experience but also hold the potential to foster community advancement and national prosperity.

Alternative Fiscal Views and Spiritual Wisdom

Black conservatives have long underscored the relationship between fiscal responsibility and ethical stewardship, a concept deeply rooted in spiritual traditions. Proverbs 22:7 teaches, *"The rich rule over the poor, and the borrower is slave to the lender."* This ancient guidance resonates strongly with alternative fiscal views which advocate for financial independence and self-reliance within the community. **By limiting debt and focusing on self-empowerment, Black conservatives echo the biblical admonishments to be prudent and wise with financial resources.**

Critique of Affirmative Action Policy through Conservative Perspectives

The critique of affirmative action policies brings to mind **the timeless principle of equality before God**. Galatians 3:28 proclaims, *"There is neither Jew nor Gentile, neither slave nor free, nor is there male and female, for you are all one in Christ Jesus."* Addressing affirmative action and similar policies from this point of view, **Black conservative thinkers have championed a vision for society that prioritizes merit and the content of one's character over racial or ethnic backgrounds**. They aspire to foster an environment wherein **each individual's achievement is the fruit of their labor and virtues**, reflecting the inherent equality bestowed upon all.

Upholding Traditional Family Structures and Free-Market Principles

The importance of the nuclear family unit cannot be overstated, especially when considering its foundation in spiritual teachings. Ephesians 5:22-23 imparts guidance on familial relationships, encapsulating the reverence that Black conservative voices ascribe to the family unit. **The nuclear family, they argue, is not merely a societal construct but a divine institution that serves as the bedrock of moral and economic stability.**

Drawing from the wellspring of theology, politics, and economics, the insights presented here advocate for a holistic approach to leading a life that honors both temporal success and spiritual reverence. Let this chapter help you find the encouragement necessary to navigate the complexities of aligning conservative principles with faith-based action.

Chapter Five

The Anomaly Myth: Embracing Conservative Black Identity

I t was a Thursday evening in a modest community town hall, where an air of simmering tension mixed with the aroma of aged wood and subtle undertones of beeswax from old, yet still vibrant, wooden pews. In the corner, rested a faintly humming piano; its keys untouched but ready to sing. The multispectral sound of ruffled papers and hushed whispers among the attendees composed a curious symphony. Here, in the heart of a southern town, where history often whispered louder than progress, James stood on the precipice of a pivotal moment, not just for himself but for his community.

James, a young Black entrepreneur, carried an aura that managed to be both gentle and unyieldingly firm. His countenance reflected the grace of his spiritual teachings, his strength cultivated through trials both in business and in life. Tonight, he was to speak about Black conservatism, a topic often met with a furrowed brow within his community. He understood the skepticism, the historical context steeped in a fight for liberation that seemed at odds with conservative principles. Yet, in his heart, James held a truth that was waiting to be acknowledged — that conservatism did not negate his identity but was an intricate part of his worldview.

As the clock's hands inched closer to the meeting's start, James centered himself, recalling the words of Proverbs 15:1, *"A gentle answer turns away wrath, but a harsh word stirs up anger."* He knew he would need this wisdom in the hours to come. As he looked around, he saw faces etched with stories of struggle and resilience, faces like those of his ancestors, whose silent strength spoke volumes.

When the town hall's gavel sounded, it was not just a call to order but a call to openness — a reminder that within these walls, every voice had the right to resonate. As James entered the space, it was as if he was walking through the pages of his history book, feeling the weight of the past as he shouldered his vision for the future.

Navigating through the crowd, he greeted his neighbors with affirming nods — his spirit exuding motivation and his demeanor reflecting his business-minded approach. "We must build, not just for ourselves but for our children and their children," he would often say. Tonight, it was about laying the cornerstones of understanding, brick by brick, for a future where diversity of thought within the Black community was seen not as a fracture, but as a fortress.

In his speech, he weaved together political insights, economic theories, and heartfelt stories from his life, each sentence a thread in the rich tapestry he presented to the audience. His tone was not of authoritarian decree but of a compassionate guide, keen to illuminate the complex landscape of identity and belief. With the cadence reserved for natural leaders, he spoke of the value in viewing conservatism through a new lens — one that honors tradition without stifling progress, cherishes liberty without disregarding the communal bond that unites a people with shared histories and dreams.

"But what does it mean for us, as a community, to embrace the full spectrum of our voices? How do we hold onto the fabric of our collective history while weaving in new patterns of thought?" With these questions lingering in the air like the final haunting notes of a hymn, James invited the room to reflect. For him, the sun had set not on a day of normalcy but on a landmark gathering that challenged and perhaps transformed perceptions. Could it be that amidst the echoes of past struggles and the foundation of faith, the seeds of inclusive dialogue and mutual respect had been sown?

Shattering the Monolith

Black conservatism is not a paradox or an oxymoron. Within the corridors of history, Black conservative thought has shaped, and continues to shape, the political landscape of America. This ideological perspective, often sidelined in the dominant liberal narrative, encompasses a spectrum of beliefs that are as integral to Black identity as any other. To fully appreciate the magnitude and validity of this stance, one must first sever the chains of misconception that bind the term "Black conservatism" to an image of betrayal or anomaly.

The roots of Black conservatism run deep, watered by the same struggles that nourish the broader Black experience. Central to this viewpoint is a profound reverence for family, faith, and self-reliance — values steeped in spiritual foundations that have long been beacons of strength for the Black community. Reflecting upon Proverbs 13:22, which states, *"A good person leaves an inheritance for their children's children,"* one can trace the conservative ethos of generational stewardship and fiscal responsibility that resonates with many.

In threading the needle of conversation around Black conservatism, we uplift stories that reveal the diversity of thought among Black Americans. By offering space for these personal narratives, including those of entrepreneurs who embody the resilience and innovation at the heart of the American Dream, we challenge monolithic characterizations. The success of these individuals, propelled by a conservative ethos, underscores the pragmatic aspect of these beliefs in business and community development.

Progress cannot be erected on a foundation of misunderstanding, and thus, dispelling the myths surrounding Black conservatism is imperative. It is an endeavor that demands a comprehensive re-evaluation of how conservative ideologies intersect with Black identity, and a firm rejection of false dichotomies suggesting that the two are incompatible. The legitimacy of conservatism within the Black experience is not a hypothesis—it is a lived reality, underscored by economic and political analyses that acknowledge the complexity of Black life in America.

In addressing the misconceptions, we also engage with the psychology of political expression within the Black community. **Consider the societal pressures that can skew perception and discourage the open declaration of conservative beliefs. To call yourself a Black conservative puts one at risk of being called an "Uncle Tom" or a "sellout", among other hurtful names, or told that "all skinfolk ain't kinfolk" by your own Black family and community.**

Reflect upon the effect — how these pressures not only stifle individual voices but can also lead to a skewing of the political representation of a diverse community. It becomes clear that for robust democratic engagement, the full range of Black voices must be heard and regarded with the sincerity they deserve.

Bridging Perspectives

These discussions serve to bridge gaps and shed light on the common ground that we all share, regardless of political leanings. The chapter instigates a dialogue that seeks to recognize the varied landscape of Black political thought. Through this acknowledgment, there emerges a powerful call to action: to **look beyond the veil of stereotypes and embrace the mosaic of Black political identities with respect and understanding.**

In aspiring to such recognition, we draw upon teachings that inspire **unity without uniformity**, celebrating the very principles of democracy. Embracing conservative Black political thought requires not just cognitive assent but also an active effort to understand its foundational premises. **We must engage with it not as an outlier, but as a legitimate reflection of the multifaceted nature of Black America.**

This approach does not suggest the erasure of differences but rather the elevation of respect for individual thought and choice. It is a path toward a society that can both revel in the melody of diverse voices and commit to a chorus that lifts every voice. In reading this chapter, readers will be equipped with the knowledge and nuance to engage in meaningful discourse, challenging the anomaly myth with the power of informed insight and empathetic understanding.

The belief that Black conservatism is incompatible with black identity has long shadowed the political landscape of America — a misapprehension that this chapter seeks to challenge head-on. The alignment of Black individuals with conservative principles is not a betrayal of racial identity but rather a reinforcement of a diverse ideological spectrum within the Black community. It's imperative to acknowledge the rich tapestry of political thought that has always existed among Black Americans, challenging the stereotype of monolithic political allegiance.

Spiritual teachings underscore the virtue of individual conscience and the pursuit of one's truth. In the context of Black conservatism, these principles mirror the Biblical exhortation that one should not be conformed to this world but be transformed by the renewal of the mind. To this end, it is about exercising the freedom to choose political beliefs that resonate with personal values, whether they be aligned with fiscal responsibility, traditional family structures, or strong national defense — values often upheld in conservative thought.

The marketplace of ideas, much like the business world, thrives on diversity and the challenge of norms. **Just as entrepreneurs are celebrated for disrupting markets with innovative thinking, so too should Black conservatives be respected for bringing a distinct viewpoint to political discussions.** These voices add necessary depth, ensuring that the community's interests are addressed in a multifaceted manner, reflective of the real range of opinions and experiences within the community itself.

In professional circles, it is well understood that the best outcomes often result from a variety of perspectives being considered and debated. Why then, should the political arena be any different for Black Americans? Each individual's life experience adds valuable insight to the collective understanding of societal issues. Practical examples abound of Black conservatives making significant contributions to political discourse, from pioneering civil rights leaders to contemporary voices that champion social progress through a conservative lens.

The virtues of personal responsibility, family cohesiveness, educational excellence, and economic empowerment run strong in Black communities. These tenets are not mere abstractions; they are interwoven in the lived experiences of countless individuals. Anchoring these commonalities within a conservative framework simply aligns with an equally valid facet of the Black experience—a facet built on achievement, self-sufficiency, and community strength.

Engaging in dialogues about Black conservatism opens the floor to a broader conversation about what it means to be Black and politically active in America. Personal anecdotes from Black conservatives often reveal a deep-seated commitment to advancing the well-being of their communities, counteracting the narratives that equate conservative beliefs with racial insensitivity. **The objective is to foster a richer, more nuanced understanding of the intersections between race and politics—a conversation where conservative Black voices are heard, contemplated, and respected.**

It's crucial to present cogent, persuasive arguments that entice readers to reevaluate longstanding assumptions about Black political identity. The essence of democracy lies in the freedom to choose — and that includes political ideologies. By illuminating the validity and historical roots of Black conservatism, we can begin to dismantle the barriers that have inhibited open conversation around this element of Black political expression.

Moving forward, it is vital to build on these reflections and delve deeper into the substance of Black conservative ideologies. Allowing the light of truth and understanding to shine on these often overlooked perspectives paves the way for a more complete, inclusive and respectful dialogue about political diversity within the Black community.

Embracing the Multifaceted Black Political Identity

Recognizing the legitimacy of conservative ideologies within the Black experience is to acknowledge the rich tapestry that makes up African American political life. Historically, Black Americans have nurtured a diverse set of values and beliefs, many of which align with principles commonly identified as conservative.

For instance, the importance of family, a strong work ethic, spiritual grounding, and the value of self-reliance are hallmarks of conservative thought that have long resonated within Black communities. These shared principles emerge not from a place of opposition to progress but from the foundational narratives that have carried many Black families through adversity and into triumph.

The Spiritual Bedrock of Black Conservatism

For many Black Americans, spirituality forms an indelible part of their heritage. Biblical teachings have often served as a source of strength and guidance, with scriptures providing solace and empowering messages of resilience. Such spiritual underpinnings dovetail with conservative ideologies that emphasize personal responsibility and moral clarity. By referencing text like Proverbs 13:22, which speaks of leaving an inheritance for one's grandchildren, one finds an echo of the conservative principle promoting financial prudence and the legacy-building that many Black families strive toward.

Entrepreneurial Spirit as a Conservative Touchstone

Within the Black community, there's a burning entrepreneurial spirit that demands recognition. It speaks to the heart of conservative values — namely, the drive for economic freedom and the pursuit of self-made success. Encouraging this entrepreneurial fire is not only motivational; it is elemental to crafting a society where individuals can thrive on their merit. Entrepreneurship requires a blend of courage, ingenuity, and a will to succeed — all qualities endorsed by conservative ideologies that also resonate deeply within a broad swath of the Black populace.

The Interplay of Economics and Justice

The Black conservative stance on economic issues often intersects with a quest for justice. The principles of free-market economics, for instance, are advanced not solely for material gain but also as a pathway to fair opportunities and empowerment. These ideologies embrace the idea that economic empowerment can serve as a catalyst for change, leveling playing fields, and breaking cycles of dependency that have historically marginalized communities.

The Courage to Persevere in Political Expression

It is essential to reflect on the effects of misconceptions, understanding that they have often muted the voices of Black conservatives. But like David facing Goliath, drawn from the heartfelt stories in the Book of Samuel, there is a call to stand with boldness, knowing that the same strength that fueled giants of our faith fuels us today. **It is time for Black conservatives to embrace their convictions with unwavering certainty**, echoing the entrepreneurial spirit that champions hard work, individual responsibility, and the power of the market to uplift all.

Every individual's political choice deserves respect, informed not by the color of their skin, but by the complexity of their experiences and the depth of their beliefs. As such, the political expression of Black conservatives must be safeguarded — a tenet critical to the true essence of liberty and the pursuit of happiness. It demands courage and persistence, both of which are hallmarks of an indomitable spirit.

Harnessing The Wisdom of Varied Disciplines

Drawing from the wells of theology, politics, and economics, we understand that the principles held by conservative Black Americans have been, and remain, deeply rational and pragmatic. These precepts align with the prosperity aimed for in the business realm, the strides toward equality envisioned by civil rights advocates, and the moral compass espoused by spiritual leaders. By weaving these strands together, one uncovers a narrative of Black conservatism that's as robust and nuanced as it is vital and compelling.

The Untapped Potential of Conservative Voices

In the arena of ideas, the voice of Black conservatism offers not just a differing perspective, but a vital contribution that can inspire change and spur innovation in political thought and policy. It is incumbent upon all who hold these values to articulate them with clarity and conviction, ensuring that they contribute meaningfully to the national discourse. **Let us therefore resolve to engage in the great conversation with the enthusiasm of a teacher eager to share, the wisdom of a mentor seasoned by experience, and the authority of a leader confident in their path.**

The value of these perspectives cannot be overstated. They enrich our collective understanding, illuminate our shared history, and guide us toward a future where every voice is heard and honored. As we continue to navigate the complex tapestry that is American politics and culture, may we do so with a deep understanding of the intrinsic worth of Black conservative thought and the contributions it will undoubtedly make to the soul and success of our nation.

Chapter Six

The Roots Run Deep: Historic Figures of Black Conservatism

T he steady hum of traffic outside the Kane family dinner table served as an ever-present reminder of the bustling world beyond. Malcolm shifted in his seat, his gaze wandering to the framed picture of Booker T. Washington on the wall. That morning, his daughter had asked about the significance of such men, and now, over a meal of baked chicken and greens, the conversation resumed. As the daylight waned, casting a golden hue through the blinds, they spoke of self-reliance and the narratives woven through the fabric of Black conservatism.

Malcolm recalled his grandfather's firm voice, steeped in the proverbs of Solomon, extolling the virtues of hard work and faith.

Echoing through time, the wisdom seemed to parallel Washington's philosophy. He pondered the path that brought him here, to the chairmanship of a local business council, striving to uplift his community through economics, echoing past doctrines.

His wife, Denise, with hands that had tended both soil and souls, listened intently, her eyes reflecting the fire of debates held long ago. She interjected with anecdotes of the Black business owners she counseled daily, underscoring her words with passages from scripture that spoke to endurance and prosperity through righteous labor.

The room was filled with the aroma of rosemary and the soft clinking of cutlery on china. Malcolm's son, a high school junior poised between adolescence and manhood, leaned forward, his countenance a study of curiosity and skepticism. The notion of past Black conservatives shaping modern dialogue impressed him, as though history had handed down a torch, its flame still casting light upon the present.

Malcolm, balancing the gravity of a teacher with the levity of a father, wove historical insights with the tactile reality of their family business. He cited examples, revealing how every ledger entry was a verse in the broader narrative of empowerment and self-determination. As dessert was served and voices melded into harmonious discourse, Malcolm reflected on his own journey — a trek that had been solitary at times, yet ever guided by the teachings of those storied forebears.

In the quiet moments following the meal, as the kitchen was being tidied and the evening's cloak began to envelop the home, Malcolm stood at the window, the city lights twinkling like distant stars, each a beacon of someone's dream. Would the core messages of those who came before lose their resonance in the age of modernity, or could the principles of Booker T. Washington and others inspire a new generation to take the reins of their own destiny?

Uncovering the Soil from Which Black Conservatism Grew

The narrative of Black conservatism often emerges as a footnote in the annals of history, yet its roots penetrate deeply into the soil of America's past. Far more than a contemporary political stance, it represents a historical continuum—a lineage that begins under the weight of adversity and blossoms into a tree whose branches shade many of today's policy debates. As we turn the pages of time, the chapter at hand seeks to illuminate the figures who sowed the seeds of self-reliance, to wander the intellectual pathways of stalwarts like Booker T. Washington, and to trace the enduring influence those proponents have in the intricate tapestry of modern political discussion.

It starts with the identification of pioneers who stood steadfast in the belief that empowerment sprang from within the individual and the community, rather than from distant institutions. Their core messages were not merely sermons of self-help but reflected a broader spiritual calling, mapping onto the biblical tenets of personal responsibility and stewardship. These early Black conservatives did not view their philosophy as diametrically opposed to the pursuit of collective uplift but rather as its most sustainable foundation.

Among these trailblazers was Booker T. Washington, an embodiment of stoic resilience and hard-earned progress. His contributions to conservative thought went beyond his own era to lay a framework for what many modern thinkers would champion as principles of economic freedom and personal agency. Washington's narratives, brimming with the virtues of education and skilled labor, urged his audiences toward a sovereign stance that transcended the constraints of their times.

As we delve into these historical narratives, we witness a legacy that persists, reverberating through decades of socio-political change. The lasting impact of historical Black conservatives can be observed vividly in the present discourse—a discourse that grapples with the intersections of race, autonomy, and governance. Here, the echoes of the past are not ghosts but guiding lights, shaping the contours of an ongoing dialogue that seeks to reconcile the pursuit of individual liberty with the quest for community advancement.

This chapter implores us to question and confront not just the nature of conservatism within the Black community but the very essence of American principles — liberty, free enterprise, and the unwavering belief in the power of the human spirit to overcome. To engage with this history is not only an exploration of political ideology but a pilgrimage to the heart of human endeavor..

When exploring the rich tapestry of Black conservatism, one must recognize the voices of early proponents who championed the principles of self-reliance and personal responsibility. These foundational ideas, deeply rooted in spiritual and moral conviction, have guided individuals in the Black community for generations.

Key among these early figures was the revered orator and writer **Frederick Douglass**. An escaped slave who became a prominent reformer, Douglass believed in the power of the Black individual to rise above circumstances through self-improvement and economic independence.

In a time when society largely sought to marginalize Black voices, Douglass's assertions struck a chord. He urged Black Americans to seize the opportunities at hand, however limited, cultivating them through diligent work and perseverance. His life itself was a testament to his beliefs, having educated himself against all odds and ultimately influencing national policies. **He asserted that reliance on self,** rather than solely on society's benevolence, would pave the way for racial uplift and integration.

Another pivotal early voice was Booker T. Washington, who emerged as a forceful proponent of Black economic advancement and self-reliance following Reconstruction. **Washington advocated for vocational training and agricultural education, believing these were the practical skills necessary for Black Americans to achieve self-sufficiency and economic security.** His founding of the Tuskegee Institute underscored his commitment to this philosophy. He contended that material progress was the keystone to improving race relations, asserting, "At the bottom of education, at the bottom of politics, even at the bottom of religion, there must be for our race, as for all races, **an economic foundation.**"

Despite criticisms from his contemporaries who disagreed with his less confrontational approach to racial equality, Washington's beliefs laid a substantial foundation for later conservative thought in the Black community. His emphasis on the importance of economic independence and education resonated across generations, advocating for individual agency amid systemic challenges.

Washington's contemporary, W.E.B. Du Bois initially supported this vision until diverging on the role of higher education and political action; a division that highlighted the diversity of thought within Black political discourse. These discussions and debates are not relics of the past but continue to inform our modern political and social landscape. Indeed, **the dialectic of self-reliance versus structural change remains a central theme in the conversation about the progress and empowerment of Black Americans.**

To truly appreciate the contribution of early Black conservatives, one must consider the economic and social context they operated within. For these individuals, self-reliance was not just philosophy, but a survival strategy in a society structured to limit Black advancement. It was a bold affirmation of faith in the resourcefulness and resilience of the Black spirit.

Such perspectives resonate in today's climate, where discussions around entrepreneurship among Black Americans often invoke these historic ideals. The narratives of Douglass and Washington serve to inspire contemporary strategies centered on financial literacy, wealth building, and innovation within Black communities. They encourage a fiercely entrepreneurial mindset, grounded in the pragmatic and moral tenets of self-help and solidarity.

As we delve deeper into the storied legacy of Black conservatism, we find these early narratives supplement current discussions in a profound way. They articulate a vision that merges personal responsibility with collective progress, suggesting that empowerment begins with the individual but doesn't end there.

Booker T. Washington and Self-Reliance

Booker T. Washington stands as a towering figure in the spectrum of Black conservatism, advocating for economic independence and education as the cornerstones of progress. He believed that self-reliance was key, and **his philosophy of "up by your own bootstraps"** was more than rhetoric — it was a credo that infused his dedication to the Tuskegee Institute and his educational practices. Washington's ethos spoke to the idea that personal responsibility and hard work were the conduits to empowerment and societal advancement.

The Atlanta Compromise: A Strategic Move

One of Washington's notable contributions was his speech at the 1895 Atlanta Exposition, known historically as the "Atlanta Compromise." **Washington proposed that Blacks should not focus on civil rights or political power, but rather on practical education and economic progress**. This stance resonated with many Black Americans who sought tangible improvements in their lives, positioning Washington as a pragmatic leader who strategically aligned with the opportunities available to his community during a time of intense racial segregation.

Vocational Education as a Pathway to Prosperity

Washington's focus on vocational education was a groundbreaking departure from traditional academic learning. By advocating for this, he recognized the immediate need for economic self-sufficiency within the Black community. **His push for industrial education was a calculated effort to equip Black individuals with the necessary skills to not only survive but also thrive in a post-slavery, yet still oppressive society.** Ironically, at the time of this writing, Washington's advocacy of vocational education still resonates today in comparison to a more expensive liberal arts education.

Moral Uplift and Economic Autonomy

An often-overlooked aspect of Washington's philosophy is **his emphasis on character building and moral righteousness**. Character, for Washington, was inextricably linked to professional success. **He**

championed virtues such as diligence, cleanliness, and thrift, which he believed were essential to economic autonomy. Washington's message was clear: moral fortitude was just as important as economic progress.

Bridging Spirituality and Self-Sufficiency

Washington infused his teachings with spiritual references that not only resonated with the deeply religious Black community but also emphasized the divine sanction of self-help principles. **By interweaving Biblical principles of stewardship and hard work, he championed a worldview where spiritual growth complemented economic ambition**. This respect for spirituality as a support system within the ambit of conservatism gave additional credence to his ethos.

Impact on Black Entrepreneurship

Booker T. Washington's legacy in Black entrepreneurship cannot be understated. His encouragement of self-reliance and skill development led to the birth of numerous Black-owned businesses. Washington saw entrepreneurship as a powerful means of combating economic disenfranchisement and pitched it as an avenue through which Black Americans could forge their own economic destinies.

Fostering Practical Alliances

Washington's advocacy was not just about internal community development but also about fostering alliances. **He understood the complexities of race relations and sought to navigate them by finding common ground with white sponsors who could assist**

in the economic upliftment of Black Americans. This controversial approach garnered support that fueled educational initiatives, laying a foundation for racial cooperation in the economic realm.

A Measured Approach to Civil Rights

When considering civil liberties, Washington took a long-term, incremental approach. He posited that economic strength would gradually lead to an improvement in civil rights for Black Americans. While criticized by some contemporaries for appearing to capitulate to segregationists, his perspective was that economic independence would eventually pave the way to full societal integration and equality.

Each of these facets of Washington's philosophy is a thread in the rich tapestry of Black conservatism — a tradition that continues to influence and inspire modern political thought and policy. As we explore the lasting impact of historical Black conservatives, it's essential to recognize and learn from the strategies they employed to navigate and transform the challenging landscapes of their eras.

The Legacy of Historical Black Conservatism

The influence of early Black conservative figures extends beyond the boundaries of their own era, planting seeds that have blossomed into a significant portion of modern political dialogue. Historical Black conservatives such as Booker T. Washington preached the virtues of self-reliance and economic independence, a message that resonates loudly in today's conversations around empowerment and success within the Black community. Their advocacy for practical education and entrepreneurship laid the groundwork for current discussions on the role of personal responsibility and community development in achieving wealth creation and racial equality.

In politics, the principles of Black conservatism have continued to shape perspectives and policy. The push for fiscal responsibility, smaller government, and individual liberty can be seen in the beliefs and actions of contemporary Black conservative leaders. They derive strength from the history of self-determination that Washington and others extolled. This historical lineage provides modern Black conservatives with a foundation of intellectual tradition to stand upon as they navigate the often tumultuous waters of current ideological battles.

Spirited Teachings in Politics and Economics

Drawing upon spiritual teachings, the historic figures of Black conservatism often emphasized that moral strength and ethical conduct were the bedrock of both personal progress and societal advancement. Scriptures that speak to honesty, diligence, and service to others are echoed in the entrepreneurial spirit that these figures championed. Their reliance on moral tenets has fortified the argument that economic growth and character development go hand in hand, a concept that has been integrated into modern movements that merge spiritual values with economic strategies.

Inheriting this blend of theology and economics, modern Black conservatives continue to advocate for policies and practices that reflect a spiritually-grounded approach to governance and commerce. By intertwining faith with the virtues of the free market and individual initiative, they argue for an ethical framework that underpins economic decisions, suggesting that fiscal conservatism is not just strategically sound but morally aligned with spiritual principles.

The Entrepreneurial Call to Action

On the business front, the legacy of past Black conservative stalwarts has served as a rallying cry for African American entrepreneurial endeavors. They serve as a testament to what can be accomplished through tenacity and business acumen. The message is clear: to harness your potential, ignite your ambition, and take command of your economic destiny. Instances of small business successes and self-made individuals are celebrated within this ideology, reminding modern audiences of the timeless value found in pursuing their goals with unrelenting drive.

Beyond mere words, this legacy provides a playbook for African Americans to follow – demonstrating **how to assert economic independence despite systemic barriers**. Today's Black entrepreneurs are encouraged to draw from the well of historical knowledge and apply those lessons to their contemporary pursuits, making the wisdom of their predecessors actionable in modern contexts.

A Testament to Political Diversity

While historical Black conservatism planted the seeds for various economic and social movements, it has also greatly enriched the political tapestry of Black America. It serves as a testament to the diversity within the community, challenging the monolithic portrayal that often dominates media and scholarly discourse. The existence of a conservative lineage among African Americans underscores the multifaceted nature of political thought in Black history, highlighting a tradition that values spirited debate and a multitude of voices.

By acknowledging this heritage, we provide space for a wider range of Black political thought leaders to be recognized and respected. This recognition allows for a more nuanced conversation about what it means to be Black and conservative, opening dialogues about the interplay between race, politics, and personal philosophy in America's social fabric.

Impact on Modern Conservatism

The narratives of historical Black conservatives have an undeniably powerful role in shaping the greater conservative movement. **Their tales of overcoming adversity and structural challenges speak to key tenets of the conservative ethos – self-help, limited governmental intrusion, and the primacy of the family unit.** At a fundamental level, the ideals espoused by the likes of Booker T. Washington have become ingrained into the rhetoric and strategy of conservative politics, **aiding in the crafting of appeals to voters across racial lines.**

By affirming the value of hard work and independence, historical Black conservatives have contributed to defining conservatism's core appeal – an appeal that continues to resonate with a segment of the Black population today. They underscore the reality that the aspirations of Black Americans are not homogeneous and that conservatism, in various forms, has played and continues to play a role in the Black American pursuit of happiness and prosperity.

Nurturing an Understanding Connection

The tradition of historical Black conservatism invites those invested in this ideology to draw parallels with the past while

crafting a vision for the future. The experiences shared by early Black conservative leaders provide relatable stories that connect generations. **As an eager entrepreneur learns from the discipline and pragmatism of Booker T. Washington, or a young politician draws inspiration from the stern resolve of a Frederick Douglass, there's a sense that the baton is being passed – an ongoing relay of ideals that link the past, present, and future.**

It is through the weaving of these personal tales and the legacies they hold that modern Black conservatives find their place within a storied continuum. This bridge between eras fosters a sense of historical grounding, encouraging today's individuals to craft their paths in the light of the rich legacies that precede them.

Forging Ahead with Clarity and Certainty

As we examine the influence of historical Black conservative figures, let us do so with an instructive voice that leaves no doubt about their impact. They have not only shaped Black America's political identity but have also offered a blueprint for personal, family and communal empowerment. The importance of their contributions to the broader American narrative cannot be overstated; their ideologies continue to inform the political strategies and individual aspirations of many within the Black community and beyond.

As advocates for a return to these foundational principles, Black conservatives today walk in the footsteps of giants. With clarity and purpose, they carry with them a powerful legacy as they forge ahead in the landscape of American politics and discourse. Their voices, steeped in a proud history of resilience and self-determination, are crucial in the continuing dialogue about the direction of the Black community and the nation as a whole.

The Legacy of Self-Reliance and Spiritual Resolve

The precepts of historic Black conservatism continue to echo in the political landscape, anchored deeply in the wisdom of self-reliance and economic independence. **These tenets mirror the teachings found in Proverbs 10:4, which tells us that "lazy hands make for poverty, but diligent hands bring wealth."** This principle of industriousness has been a guiding light for many, showing us the path toward personal growth and community development. **As these early proponents preached, success stems not from dependence on others, but from the intestinal fortitude to carve one's own destiny.**

Booker T. Washington's contributions stand as a testament to these ideals. He not only espoused them but also lived them, becoming a symbol of what African Americans could achieve through education and entrepreneurship. His vision materialized through the Tuskegee Institute, which continues to shape young minds today. His insights remind us that to uplift a community, we must start by fortifying its individuals with knowledge, morality and opportunity.

Our understanding of the impactful messages from these historical figures is not a mere academic exercise; it is a call to action. **To honor their legacy, we must not only reflect on their words but also embody their teachings.** Our modern political dialogue can be enriched by revisiting these enduring messages, which encourage us to confront challenges with a mix of self-sufficiency and spiritual fortitude.

Economic Empowerment Through Action

The journey to economic empowerment is one filled with obstacles, yet it is a path well paved by those who came before us. These trailblazers have shown us that the pursuit of entrepreneurship is not just about financial returns; it is about upholding dignity and securing economic autonomy. In a climate that often underestimates the potential within Black communities, the lessons of our predecessors illuminate the possibilities that arise from embracing commerce and innovation. When we start businesses, invest in education, and support our own, we carry forward a legacy of empowerment that can resonate for generations.

A Reservoir of Wisdom for the Future

Our experience serves as a well of knowledge from which we can draw practical and actionable advice. Reflecting on my own journey, I recall the times when the principles of Black conservatism provided a compass in moments of uncertainty. It was the unwavering belief in personal responsibility and community engagement that guided decisions and cultivated resilience. In echoing these values, we do more than preserve history; we activate it within our lives.

Let us approach the future with the assurance that our roots have weathered storms and our branches are strong enough to bear the weight of new challenges. **We are called upon to be stewards of this conservative heritage, molding it with the clay of contemporary insights while keeping the core tenets intact.** Our mindful application of these values will shape a society that respects individual merit and nurtures the entrepreneurial spirit.

A Synergy of Disciplines for a Richer Perspective

A profound understanding comes from synthesizing key insights from theology, politics, and economics, creating a multifaceted lens through which we can examine the legacy of Black conservatism. Stories of success are not merely tales to be told but blueprints with real-world applications. As we dissect these narratives, let us apply the same fervor to our own ventures, enriching our discourse and actions with the lessons of our history.

This narrative is not limited to a single perspective but is augmented by the contributions from diverse fields. By understanding the economic theories that underpin self-sufficiency and the political frameworks that support individual liberties, we craft richer, more holistic strategies for progress. This intersectionality is crucial, as it molds our approach to tackling today's issues with the wisdom of years past.

Engaging in Personal Dialogues

Imagine sitting down with a mentor, someone wise in the ways of life and business, sharing personal stories that resonate with truth and inspiration. This is the atmosphere we aim to cultivate as we explore the influence of historic Black conservatism. When we share these narratives, our connection deepens, and the lessons become more profound, etching themselves into our collective memory and individual ambitions.

In receiving this shared wisdom, we move beyond the role of passive readers to active participants in a dialogue that can spur us to reach new heights and forge our own paths. Let us harness the spirit of our ancestors, who carved out a space for their voices and visions, and do the same in our ventures and communities.

Communicating With Clarity and Conviction

To weave a tapestry of understanding, we must use language that is both eloquent and accessible. Our mission is to inform and engage, and this requires precision in our expression. We must articulate the value and importance of these historic messages with a certainty that can bolster conviction in our readers.

As your guide through this narrative, it is my responsibility to illuminate these transformative ideas with clarity and to inspire you to reflect upon and integrate these principles into your own lives. **Let these historical portraits of conservatism not be static images of the past but vibrant influences that shape our present actions and future aspirations.**

Chapter Seven

A Spectrum Within: The Diversity of Black Conservative Thought

The sun was setting on Atlanta, casting a warm golden hue over the bustling city as Marcus walked through the streets. He was a man of sturdy build, carrying the complexities of his intellectual pursuits silently on his shoulders like the briefcase in his hand — wearied leather, worn from carrying papers filled with the musings of economic disparities and social philosophies. His stride was steady, a rhythm learned on the pavements of his youth, streets that whispered tales of prosperity and hardship in equal measure.

Marcus had spent years studying the world of Black conservatism, his mind a chamber of debates between tradition, libertarian ideals, and religious convictions. That evening, as he headed towards a speaking engagement, the weight of these responsibilities was heavier than usual. He reflected on the various schools of thought, the respect they each demanded, and how they addressed the socio-economic challenges faced by the Black community. Traditional conservatives emphasized structure and self-sufficiency, while libertarians called for minimal government intervention. Then there were those driven by faith, seeing moral revival as the key to progress.

With each step, he considered his audience, the young entrepreneurs hungry for direction and understanding. He knew they sought strategies for success amidst systemic barriers, looking to him for wisdom — a modern-day sage dressed in the garb of a scholar. They were creating something new in a world that often seemed content with the old, their businesses a beacon of innovation reflecting their perseverant spirits.

Inside the conference hall, Marcus's eyes scanned the room. This was an assembly of minds, radiant with the hope of youth and the sharpness of ambition. His heart understood their concerns and their searching for more than just profit but purpose.

He spoke with gravitas, his voice a calm stream of clarity amongst the babble of nervous anticipation. He infused his speech with spiritual principles, quoting Proverbs to emphasize the reward of diligence and integrity in business. His anecdotes of personal triumph and the occasional setback served as a testament to the value of resilience — lessons from the pulpit to the marketplace, now to the public square.

As the evening gave way to discussion, Marcus felt the familiar swell of pride in facilitating a meeting of minds, a confluence of tradition and aspiration. The participants leaned in, their questions thought-provoking, their gaze intent. They discussed strategies and economic models, the room a symphony of voices each articulating their piece of the intricate puzzle.

In one corner of the room, a young woman debated the role of the government in providing opportunities. Her eyes were fierce with the fire of libertarianism, yet she listened intently as Marcus explained the need for balance, the art of charting a course that married liberty with community.

The room was abuzz long after Marcus finished speaking. He stepped outside, the city's night sky now a canvas of darkness punctuated by the city's lights. As he walked towards his car, he contemplated the future of these young souls and their ventures. How would they navigate the narrow path between self-reliance and the acknowledgement of systemic obstacles? How would their faith, their individualism, and their cultural heritage intertwine to create ventures that were robust and yet sensitive to the community's needs?

Marcus felt as though he had sown seeds, fertile ideas on the rich soil of eager minds. But the harvest was not his to reap. The true question lingered, floating on the cool night air, pregnant with the promise of tomorrow: What roads would they carve for themselves from the crossroads of these ideologies?

The Labyrinth of Ideological Diversity

The multifaceted landscape of black conservatism in America is a testament not only to political diversity but to the resilient spirit of human intellect and moral inquiry. Understanding the spectrum of black conservative thought requires an excavation of ideologies that reach beyond the monolithic representation often depicted in contemporary media discourse. Traditional, libertarian, and religious viewpoints weave through the fabric of black conservatism, each with its unique narrative and interpretation of socio-economic challenges. The adhesive that binds these divergent streams is a profound commitment to individual liberty, personal responsibility, and an unwavering belief in the virtuosity of faith-infused principles.

Each strand of black conservative thought dutifully addresses the socio-economic hurdles facing communities, yet they do so from varied philosophical starting points. The traditionalist might argue from a standpoint grounded in historical interpretation and a steadfast adherence to constitutional originalism. Libertarian wings advocate for minimal state intervention, trusting in the autonomous power of the free market and the sovereign individual to birth innovation and economic prosperity. On another front, religious conservatives draw upon spiritual teachings, fusing moral guidance from sacred texts with political philosophy in their approach to community and statesmanship.

These differences in approach highlight the complex ideological fabric under the umbrella of black conservatism. It is an ecosystem where the role of government, understanding of freedom, and pathways to equality take on different shades, reflecting an intricate interplay between faith, reason, and experience. Grappling with these ideologies demands both an appreciation of their uniqueness and a recognition of the shared aspirations for a prosperous, just society they collectively seek to manifest.

The insights gained from exploring this domain are not merely academic; they offer tangible strategies for engaging with socio-economic challenges. They propose practical solutions, from entrepreneurial empowerment to robust community engagement, stressing the importance of action over rhetoric. Just as the Proverbs counsel diligence and shrewdness in one's work, so too do black conservative thinkers emphasize the virtues of industriousness and ingenuity in crafting a more fulfilling life and a robust community.

Engaging with the diversity of black conservative thought is comparable to entering into a dialogue with a rich lineage of maverick thinkers who offer real-world experience and actionable advice. It is to have a seat at a table where past trials and triumphs inform the plans of today and the strategies for tomorrow. Of paramount importance in this dialogue is respect for the spiritual essence of the black conservative tradition — a reverence for its power to inspire, equip, and sustain those who subscribe to its tenets.

Empowerment leaks from the texts of black conservative voices like ink on paper, **imparting the belief that despite systemic adversities, internal fortitude and faith-driven initiative can pave the way towards greater self-reliance, social mobility, and equality.** It is within this empowering narrative that the lessons of black conservatism often resonate most profoundly with those who seek not just to understand the world, but to actively shape it.

This chapter is a call to action to look beyond the surface and perceive the intricate web of intellect and spirituality that is the mark of black conservatism. It encourages the reader to appreciate the intricate patterns woven by its thinkers — patterns which, when traced, unveil comprehensive blueprints for addressing societal challenges through the perspectives of faith, freedom, and fiscal responsibility. Through a multifaceted lens, we see a gamut of ingenuity, from grassroots community transformation to the heights of policy-making. It is in these details that we discover the true vitality and potency of black conservative philosophy.

The tapestry of black conservative thought is as multicolored as it is historical, offering a variety of perspectives that address the needs and aspirations of black Americans through a conservative lens. Within this spectrum, three more prominent and distinct schools of thought — traditional, libertarian, and religious conservatism — each bring forth unique philosophies that underpin their respective ideologies.

Traditional black conservatism places a strong emphasis on self-reliance, entrepreneurial success, and educational achievement as the pillars of progress. Traditionalists advocate for the power of the free market, personal responsibility, and a minimally intrusive government as essential to the prosperity of not just black Americans, but of all individuals within a society. These tenets are rooted in a belief that the path to empowerment and dignity lies through economic independence and moral rectitude.

Moving on to **libertarian black conservatism**, this school of thought elevates the primacy of individual liberties and limited government intervention to the forefront of its values. The libertarian wing often argues that smaller government and free market principles provide the best environment for personal empowerment and collective community advancement. They champion civil liberties, property rights, and fiscal conservatism, and are often skeptical of government's role in dealing with social issues, positing that community-led solutions are more effective and less prone to abuse and incompetence.

In contrast, **religious black conservatism** intertwines spiritual beliefs with political ideology, holding that moral guidance derived from faith is essential to the structure and order of society. This perspective emphasizes the importance of traditional family values, the sanctity of life and marriage, and the role that religious institutions play in community support and development. For followers of this school, political and social policies should be aligned with religious teachings, and the moral compass provided by faith is seen as a critical counterbalance to secular influences.

Each school, while distinct, shares an overarching commitment to advancing the standing of black Americans. Yet, how they propose to address socio-economic challenges varies considerably. Traditional conservatives may prioritize initiatives like school choice or entrepreneurship programs, whereas libertarians would argue for deregulation and tax reform to stimulate business and personal liberty. Religious conservatives, on the other hand, might focus on community-driven and social programs that align with their faith-based values to provide support to those in need.

While it is tempting to view black conservatism as a monolith, the reality is far more complex. This diversity of thought provides a rich dialog within the community, offering varying strategies and solutions for the socio-economic issues that black Americans face. Engaging with the philosophy of each school of thought reveals a profound reverence for the potential of the individual and the community, tied to the belief that conservative principles can foster the advancement of black Americans.

Such an understanding enriches the broader conversation around African American politics, allowing us to move beyond simplistic binaries and appreciate the nuanced perspectives that drive political decision-making. This acknowledgment is vital in crafting policies that resonate with the varied priorities of black conservatives and indeed, the entire black community.

As we delve deeper into black conservative thought, we discover ideas grounded in real-world experience and intellectual rigor, as well as a fervent belief in the possibilities of America. The examples set forth by maverick thinkers and activists from these varying schools illuminate the entrepreneurial spirit and moral clarity that define this segment of the political spectrum.

Moving forward, the challenge lies in harmonizing these differing ideologies into a cohesive strategy that addresses the practicalities of governing, while maintaining the integrity of each school's principles. As we explore the ways in which these perspectives address socio-economic challenges in the following section, we must keep in mind the richness of the black conservative heritage and the potential it holds for shaping the future.

The Tapestry of Economic Thought among Black Conservatives

Black conservatives approach socio-economic challenges through a variety of lenses, reflecting the diversity within their ranks. For example, the **traditional conservatives** within the Black community often champion the virtues of free markets, advocating for policies that promote entrepreneurial spirit and personal responsibility. They argue that by reducing regulatory barriers and encouraging small business ownership, economic disparities can be mitigated and prosperity can be attained, irrespective of race. Here lies a call to action for Black individuals to seize the reins of economic opportunity, where perseverance and hard work are pathways to financial independence and wealth creation.

The **libertarian segment** of Black conservatism is distinguished by its strong emphasis on limited government intervention. These thinkers advocate for a fundamental restructuring of socio-economic paradigms, calling for the protection of individual liberties and property rights. They argue that by fostering a climate where ingenuity and competition can thrive without excessive government overreach, an efficient allocation of resources will naturally correct economic imbalances. This perspective is rooted in the belief that personal liberty is the cornerstone of economic empowerment.

Religious perspectives within Black conservatism tend to focus on community support structures informed by spiritual teachings. Such **faith-based conservative thinkers** lean on principles derived from respected spiritual texts, including the Bible, using them as a moral compass and worldview to address socio-economic challenges. They emphasize family unity, strong work ethics, and altruism as necessary components of a prosperous society. By advocating for social policies that align with these values, they aim to uplift individuals and bridge the divide between poverty and opportunity.

Addressing Socio-Economic Disparities with Policy and Principles

Proposed solutions to socio-economic issues among these diverse strains of Black conservatism often intersect with public policy. For instance, traditional conservatives may support tax reforms that incentivize business investment in underprivileged communities, thereby sparking local job creation. Libertarian-inclined conservatives frequently suggest that dismantling the welfare state would decrease dependency and invigorate a culture of self-sufficiency.

Meanwhile, religious conservatives commonly endorse community-centered programs that support entrepreneurship while also addressing educational and moral development. Consider the impact of faith-based initiatives that partner with local businesses to provide job training – these programs can be bridges to economic self-reliance, reflecting a merger of spiritual guidance and practical skill-building.

The Entrepreneurial Ethos in Black Conservative Discourse

The emphasis on entrepreneurship is particularly palpable in the Black conservative dialogue on socio-economic advancement. Fostering an environment where Black-owned businesses can flourish is seen as a powerful driver for economic uplift and social mobility. Traditional conservatives in the community frequently tout the success stories of Black entrepreneurs as examples of what can be achieved through ingenuity and persistence. This narrative reinforces the idea that business acumen, coupled with a strong sense of autonomy, can serve as a steady solution against residual systemic barriers.

Real-World Application of Black Conservative Economic Strategies

Practical examples abound where Black conservative economic principles have been put into practice. Consider the case of urban revitalization projects spearheaded by Black conservative entrepreneurs who leverage tax incentives to rebuild and empower local, historically black neighborhoods. Such initiatives counter the narrative of dependency with one of partnership and self-empowerment, demonstrating the real-world efficacy of conservative economic thought in addressing social challenges.

Moreover, educational choice stands as another battleground where Black conservatives seek to improve socio-economic outcomes. Advocacy for charter schools, more parental involvement, and voucher programs is predicated on the conviction that a robust education, tailored to the needs of the individual families of the community, can equalize opportunities across socio-economic divides.

The Role of Mentorship and Community Empowerment

In grappling with socio-economic challenges, the value of mentorship and community empowerment is frequently underscored by Black conservatives of all stripes. They argue that **sustainable economic growth stems from nurturing the potential within the community, with established figures guiding and supporting emerging talents**. In the business realm, this translates into successful Black entrepreneurs leading by example, providing mentorship, and opening networks to aspiring individuals. Community empowerment becomes not only a social imperative but a strategic approach to socio-economic development.

Policy as a Reflection of Conservative Principles

Policy proposals from Black conservative thinkers are often infused with their core principles. Tax credits for families that invest in education, funding for apprenticeship programs, and support for small business incubators are just a few approaches that meld conservative economic philosophy with actionable policies. While proposals vary, the unifying thread is the aim to create an infrastructure that supports self-reliance and individual prosperity, challenging the status quo and asserting the importance of economic freedom.

Bridging Economic Thought with Actionable Solutions

Regardless of the particular school of conservative thought, there is an underlying conviction that when outfitted with the right tools — be it through policy, community effort, or individual drive — Black Americans have the capacity to overcome socio-economic barriers. Ongoing dialogue that encourages the integration of diverse perspectives can help translate these ideologies into tangible programs that address socio-economic adversities in meaningful ways.

Understanding the Nuances of Black Conservative Thought

As we traverse the landscape of Black conservative thought, a distinct truth emerges: the diversity in philosophical orientations is not a matter of contradiction but of complexity. Traditional, libertarian, and religious threads within this ideology weave a rich tapestry that reflects a deep-seated intention to address socio-economic challenges in ways that honor both individual and community strengths.

In appreciating the variant schools of thought, we recognize the united goals of empowerment and prosperity. Resonating with both the past and the ambition for the future, the call for vision, integrity, and purpose in leadership and governance echoes throughout the community, summoning us to rise above mediocrity and strive for excellence.

As we move forward, **remember that the multiplicity within Black conservative ideology beckons us not to choose between perspectives but to find strength in its spectrum.** For within the kaleidoscope that is Black conservatism, lies not only the legacy of a profound ideological heritage but the seeds of inventive strategies capable of inspiring change and advancing prosperity for future generations.

Chapter Eight

Empathy and Engagement: Understanding the Black Conservative

I n the golden haze of a late afternoon, John, a Black conservative businessman, navigated the mixed feelings of anticipation and apprehension as he prepared his keynote address for a local entrepreneurship summit. His journey as a successful entrepreneur, guided by his faith and conservative values, had been both complicated and empowering. As he sifted through his notes, John reflected on how his personal experiences and the historical context of Black conservatism had shaped his views and his approach to business, hoping to impart a sense of wisdom and motivation to his audience.

John took a moment to glance out of his office window, the di-
minishing sun casting solemn shadows over his face. He remembered
passages from Proverbs, seeing diligence as the path to leadership and
prosperity, a belief that had propelled him to where he stood now.
His faith, intertwined with his ideology, reminded him that while man
plans his course, it is the Lord who establishes his steps. This duality
of human effort under divine guidance framed his worldview, diver-
sifying his conservative thinking with a touch of spiritual humility.

As the cool breeze of early evening wafted through the slatted
blinds, he considered the challenges his perspective often faced. He
pondered the juxtaposition of **being a minority within a minority**
and how this intersection shaped his push for economic independence
within his community. John believed in addressing disparities not
through dependency, but through empowerment and self-sufficiency.
"Empower a man to fish, and he can feed his community," he mur-
mured to himself, the adage echoing through his office.

Turning his swivel chair away from the mahogany desk, he re-
hearsed a motivational passage that would resonate with budding entrepreneurs — an anecdote of his first venture, riddled with obstacles,
yet overcome through perseverance and faith. He wanted to inspire
action, to fuel the entrepreneurial spirit with the warm tenor of his
words, by sharing a blueprint of resilience informed by his conservative
principles.

John's deep understanding of economic principles, blended with
political convictions, seemed relevant now more than ever. He considered how to integrate ideas from economic theorists who extolled
the virtues of free markets with the political pragmatism of conservative ideologies. By doing so, he intended to enlighten his audience
on creating opportunities within a capitalist society, underscoring the
importance of innovation and personal responsibility.

As the room dimmed, John paused to reflect on the spiritual and intellectual heritage that shaped his unique standpoint. He knew the path forward was through informed dialogue, capturing the nuances of thought that so many like him held. And as the clock ticked, signaling the approach of his speaking engagement, John questioned how his perspective could align with the spiritual and economic emancipation of his community. Would his words bridge understanding or fortify divisions? How could he ensure that the empathetic approach he desired would resonate within the diversity of Black conservative ideologies and beyond?

Bridging Divides with Empathy

To journey through the multifaceted landscape of Black conservatism is to traverse a path less recognized in modern political discourse. Yet, it is precisely this less-trodden route that offers richer insights into the dynamics of American political identity. The essence of this chapter lies in **fostering an empathetic approach to understanding the existence and experiences that shape the perspectives of Black conservatives**. It is through empathy that we can engage with these often-overlooked voices, recognizing that their stories are interwoven with the broader tapestry of American history. **The mature reader will find that empathy does not always equate to agreement, but it is the cornerstone of constructive dialogue.**

As one delves deeper into the personal narratives and historical context that give rise to Black conservative thought, it becomes evident that the movement is not monolithic. Diverse life experiences — from the inner cities to the halls of academia — mold the principles and beliefs of many Black individuals who align with conservative thought. To comprehend this faction of political identity, we must examine individual histories and the ways in which they interact with and inform such ideologies. These experiences are not isolated incidents but rather integral fragments of America's expansive political mosaic.

Furthermore, igniting informed dialogue around Black conservatism is imperative. **Far too often, conversations about Black political ideology are mired in presumption and simplification, disregarding the intricacies that underpin each individual's standpoint.** Herein lies the responsibility to move beyond gross caricatures and media sound bites, addressing the real and present nuances that characterize Black conservative thought. Debates infused with depth, curiosity, humility, compassion and nuance not only illuminate underappreciated viewpoints but also enrich the broader understanding of what it means to be a patriot in a racially and ideologically diverse society.

The task at hand extends beyond just listening. It calls for a reckoning with one's own preconceptions and a surrender to the complex reality that individuals' political alignments are often a reflection of their profound personal journeys and life experiences. Here we can employ spiritual teachings and texts to underscore the empathy required for this deeper comprehension. A passage from Proverbs 4:7 — *"Wisdom is the principal thing; therefore get wisdom: and with all thy getting get understanding"* — resonates with the undertaking to fully grasp the dimensions of Black conservatism.

Envisioning Constructive Engagement

This endeavor calls for an entrepreneurial spirit—one that is innovative and willing to build new bridges in political and social dialogue. It is paramount to apply empowerment and action, **encouraging read-**

ers to venture into engagements with Black conservatives not as adversaries but as fellow architects of our societal discourse. Opportunities for genuine enlightenment are present when conversations are approached with a readiness to learn, share, and grow, rather than simply to persuade, argue, or demonize.

Drawing from real-world experiences solidifies an expertise that transcends theoretical musings. By sharing pertinent anecdotes and citing practical examples, strategies for engagement become tangible, with actionable advice that readers can implement in their interactions. This not only conveys a deep understanding of the subject but provides a toolbox for those who seek to build effective and fruitful dialogues.

The insights offered throughout the chapter aim to chart a course that is both professional and solution-oriented. The tone embodies an approachable formality, providing clear-eyed strategies that respect the complexity of the subject while steering clear of over-simplification. By marrying experience with an academic grounding in relevant fields, from theology to economics, a well-rounded perspective emerges, offering a comprehensive understanding of the undercurrents that define Black conservatism.

Cultivating Understanding Through Personal Connection

The warmth of personal connection can illuminate the intricacies of this journey. Just as a mentor shares stories laden with wisdom, we too must embrace moments of relatability that forge a conversation among peers, fostering an atmosphere that is both genuine and insightful.

It is through this affable and authoritative dialogue that the essence of Black conservative thought is truly revealed. The narrative is crafted in a style that is both charming and commanding, speaking directly to the heart of the matter with confidence and clarity. As we explore the nuances of what it means to be a Black conservative, we craft a narrative that is neither verbose nor overly complex, ensuring that the conversation remains both accessible and thought-provoking.

Ultimately, the goal is to persuade through clarification, firmly asserting and articulating the value of understanding Black conservative perspectives and their relation to the black community. The instructive voice adopted herein commands attention to the salient points, ensuring that each reader comes away enlightened and equipped to partake in a richer, more inclusive political conversation.

Empathy is not merely a warm sentiment; **it is a foundational principle that allows us to understand perspectives divergent from our own**. This is especially relevant when approaching the dialogue surrounding Black conservatism. **To truly engage with Black conservative perspectives, we must first seek to listen deeply and comprehend the experiences behind these viewpoints. An empathetic approach does not mean we forfeit our beliefs and convictions, but rather that we respect the journey and reasoning that have shaped others' convictions.**

Let's consider the spiritual dimension of empathy, which can be found across various religious teachings. In Christianity, for instance, the Bible encourages believers in Philippians 2:4 not to look out only for their interests but also for the interests of others. This scriptural mandate suggests that genuine engagement with others, including Black conservatives, requires a willingness to consider their experiences as valuable and instructive.

In a business context, empathy is a powerful tool for leadership and problem-solving. A leader who can understand the motivations and concerns of their team is better equipped to inspire and guide them toward common goals. In the same way, engaging with Black conservative perspectives involves recognizing the legitimate concerns and aspirations they address, such as the importance of individual responsibility, the value of free enterprise, and the role of tradition and family in building strong communities.

From a professional viewpoint, consider the value of diverse experiences. Innovation often springs from the cross-pollination of different ideas and practices. The discourse on Black conservatism provides a compelling case study of how divergent historical narratives and cultural experiences can inform political ideologies. This intellectual diversity enhances our collective understanding and helps us to devise more nuanced strategies for tackling socio-political issues.

Acknowledging Growth and Change

For many Black conservatives, their ideological stance might be a result of generational wisdom, cultural values, and / or responses to contemporary societal trends. By sharing personal narratives, we can appreciate the complex mosaic that informs Black conservative thought, which is often rooted in a history of resilience and a quest for self-determination. Such narratives underscore the need to approach conservatism in the Black community not as a monolith but as a spectrum of experiences and convictions.

In discussing the intersection of theology, politics, and economics, **it's important to avoid reducing complex individuals to mere representatives of ideologies**. Black conservatism cannot be understood in isolation but must be located within the broader narrative of Black historical struggles and triumphs, the evolution of American society, and the dynamic landscape of global economics. The interplay of these fields provides a richer, more informative backdrop against which Black conservative thought can be explored and appreciated.

Effective discourse relies on a warm, personal exchange, where participants feel heard and valued. The conversation about Black conservatism should echo this atmosphere, **encouraging an open exchange of ideas rather than a combative rebuttal of positions. It's an opportunity to learn from each other, to dismantle stereotypes, and to discover the multifaceted nature of political identity within the Black community.**

To convey understanding, use language that bridges gaps rather than widens them. When discussing Black conservatism, choose words that resonate with shared values, such as family, community, and liberty. This helps to position the dialogue not as an adversarial debate but as a mutual exploration of ideas that hold personal significance, establish common ground, and foster opportunities for collaboration for societal impact.

Fostering Inclusive Dialogue for Deeper Insight

To truly understand the ideologies of Black conservatives, one must examine how personal experiences and historical context shape their perspectives. Black conservatism, often seen as contradictory in light of the historical struggle for civil rights, is in fact a multifaceted ideology that finds its roots in the same pursuit for equality and autonomy. The values of self-reliance and economic independence that many Black conservatives espouse can be traced back to leaders such as Frederick Douglass and Booker T. Washington, who emphasized education and entrepreneurship as means of advancement.

Spiritual principles have traditionally played a significant role in shaping Black conservative thought. Scriptures and religious teachings reinforce the values of hard work, perseverance, and ethical behavior — qualities embraced by many within the movement. By aligning life choices with faith-driven principles and a Judeo-Christian worldview, many Black conservatives often strive to create a society where freedom of religion and moral responsibility guide social and political actions. This intersection of faith and politics is not just theoretical but deeply rooted in the lived experiences of individuals who have found solace and strength in their spiritual beliefs and walks of faith.

Empowerment Through Entrepreneurship

There is often a strong entrepreneurial spirit among Black conservatives, born out of a desire to overcome systemic barriers and achieve economic prosperity on their own terms. This can be seen as a modern expression of a historic ethos—dating from the days when Black business districts thrived during the era of segregation. There is an understanding that economic strength is a cornerstone of freedom and self-determination. Motivational anecdotes of Black entrepreneurs who have succeeded against the odds serve not only as inspiration but as tangible proof of the power of self-initiative and enterprise in fostering empowerment.

Real-world experience plays a major role in the conservative dialogue. For instance, individuals who have climbed the socioeconomic ladder, often against considerable obstacles, provide powerful testimony to the potential of free-market principles and personal endeavor. Their successes and the strategies that facilitated their upward mobility offer actionable advice for others seeking similar paths to model and replicate.

While discussing Black conservative ideologies, it is helpful to maintain a professional and business-oriented tone. **Refrain from**

**the strategies of the opposition that resort to constant inter-
ruption, name-calling, and dismissive tactics that degrade both
the idea and the person subscribing to such an idea.** Strategies and
solutions for socioeconomic advancement must be precisely articulated — no less important than in any corporate boardroom or public
forum televised to the masses. It is about providing pragmatic advice
and empowering others to take action that can change their lives and
communities for the better.

Integrating insights from various fields offers a more comprehensive understanding of Black conservatism. Concepts from theology
highlight the moral and ethical framework, economic theories explain the advocacy for market-based solutions, and political science
elucidates the preference for policies that promote individual liberty.
**This amalgamation of insights creates a narrative that reflects a
well-rounded, intellectual tradition within Black conservatism,**
echoing voices like those of Thomas Sowell, Walter E. Williams, Larry
Elder, Shelby Steele and Jason L. Riley, who delve into the cultural,
economic, and political dimensions of the ideology.

The Personal Connect

**Creating a warm and personal atmosphere is crucial when dis-
cussing an ideology that is deeply personal for many.** Sharing
experiences of overcoming hardships or witnessing the positive impact
of conservative policies on individuals and families allows for a connection that transcends political rhetoric. It brings the human element
to the forefront, accentuating the impact that ideas have on real lives.

The charm of a conversation-like narrative lies in its power to **engage without alienating**. Through earnest discussions about personal responsibility, the importance of family, and the role of the state,

this approach demystifies Black conservative thought. It retains the authority born of experience and study while inviting readers into an insightful exchange of ideas, mirroring the enthusiasm of a knowledgeable teacher without becoming didactic.

Accessibility is key in communicating complex political ideologies. Opting for simplicity over verbosity ensures that the principles and tenets of Black conservatism are comprehensible to a wider audience. This strategy is particularly important when countering misconceptions and stereotypes that often surround the Black conservative movement.

Persuasion is a subtle art, but in unpacking the value and importance of Black conservative ideologies, it becomes essential to be forthright and confident. Constructing arguments that are informed and poignant bolsters the reader's understanding and appreciation of the perspectives being presented. This solidifies the significance of the ideology within the broader political landscape and within the rich tapestry of Black political thought.

The instructive voice is employed when it's necessary to highlight critical points. Emphasizing the foundation upon which Black conservative ideologies are built requires a commanding tone that draws the reader's focus to the essence of these beliefs. This includes reverence for the family unit, dedication to faith, and commitment to educational and economic success as pillars of societal advancement.

Fostering Dialogue Integrating Diverse Perspectives

Engaging in informed dialogue is essential when exploring the nuances of Black conservative thought. It involves a willingness to listen and an openness to understanding the multiple facets that drive individual ideologies. As we move forward, we must acknowledge that Black conservative perspectives are not a monolith but rather a mosaic of experiences and beliefs. Historical context, personal experiences, and individual values play a formidable role in shaping these ideologies. Therefore, fostering a dialogue, entrenched in curiosity and respect, can bridge gaps and unearth common ground among people who think, believe, and vote differently from each other.

To effectively engage in conversations about Black conservatism, one must **approach the topic with both humility and inquisitiveness.** By examining how conservative principles align with the aspirations and the moral compass of individuals within the Black community, we can begin to understand the appeal of these ideologies. For many, the conservative emphasis on self-reliance, entrepreneurial spirit, and family values resonates deeply. These are not just political stances but also deeply spiritual beliefs that mirror the ethics found in many religious teachings.

Applying Scriptural Frameworks to Political Discourse

The integration of faith into political discourse often shapes Black conservative thought. Passages from respected spiritual texts can be used as a framework for understanding the moral imperatives that many Black conservatives adhere to. For instance, principles of stewardship and community resonate strongly within this group, reflecting a desire to uphold the biblical mandates of honesty, integrity, and hard work. By aligning the conversation with these timeless spiritual ideals, we can engage in discussions that transcend mere politics, touching on the core values that define one's worldview.

Personal responsibility and fiscal stewardship are also pivotal themes running through the Black conservative ideology. Recall the parable of the talents (Matthew 25:14-30), which encourages individuals to multiply the gifts bestowed upon them. This parable can serve as a metaphor for the commitment to self-reliance towards upward mobility and socio-economic advancement — a commitment that can be found coursing through the veins of Black conservatism.

Illuminating the Entrepreneurial Spirit

The entrepreneurial mindset, a cornerstone of Black conservative values, demands attention in any dialogue about this political spectrum. Many Black conservatives view entrepreneurship as a direct path to empowerment and freedom. Celebrating success stories within the Black community provides tangible evidence of the power of hard work and innovation. These narratives, rich with personal anecdotes and practical examples, are not just inspiring — they're instructive. They illuminate pathways for others to follow, underscoring the importance of perseverance, hoping to inspire a generation brimming with business aspirations.

To truly capture these nuances, it's crucial to promote real-life examples. We should not merely quote statistics but also highlight individual achievements and case studies that offer a roadmap for others. By celebrating these milestones, we reinforce the message that achievement and self-sufficiency are within reach for every individual, irrespective of their background.

Nurturing Economic Self-Sovereignty

Black conservatism often emphasizes economic independence as a key component of freedom and self-determination. It is vital to explore how fiscal responsibility and financial literacy form the backbone of this ideology. In discussions about Black conservative thought, we must integrate conversations about debt repayment, the importance of both insurance and investments for family stability, small business ownership, upskilling of talents and skills for tomorrow's economic needs, wealth creation, asset protection and intergenerational wealth transfer — topics that are fortified with economic theory yet grounded in practical, everyday strategies.

We should heed lessons from successful business leaders and economists who embody the principles that Black conservatives advocate for. Their expertise and experiences can provide actionable advice and serve as a reminder that the pursuit of economic empowerment is both a personal journey and a collective mission.

Incorporating Diverse Disciplinary Insights

A well-rounded discussion about Black conservative thought naturally includes insights from politics and economics, but it equally benefits from the integration of theology, sociology, and cultural studies. This interdisciplinary approach enriches the dialogue and enables us to see the interconnections between different facets of life. Theories from these domains can be used to explain the holistic nature of Black conservatism, which often interweaves spiritual convictions with pragmatic considerations.

As we articulate these nuances, it's paramount to remain grounded in reality while providing fodder for elevated thought. By incorporating case studies and examples from various fields, we provide a concrete context for abstract theories and encourage a more comprehensive examination of what drives Black conservative ideals.

Engaging the Depths of Personal Experience

The power of personal storytelling cannot be overstated in conversations about political beliefs. When delving into Black conservative thought, we must acknowledge and respect the deeply personal experiences that inform these views. By sharing these stories, we foster empathy and offer perspectives that might otherwise be overlooked. We begin to **see the individual — not just the ideology — as a complex tapestry woven from personal life experiences, past education, and both spiritual and secular influences.**

In these narratives, we discover the reasons why conservatism may resonate on a personal level — whether it's an emphasis on a strong family, a commitment to safeguarding freedoms and protecting our neighborhoods, or an entrepreneurial dream realized. These personal reflections lend authenticity to the dialogue and build a bridge of understanding that extends far beyond political stereotypes.

Sowing Seeds of Productive Engagement

Ultimately, our goal is to sow seeds for productive and meaningful engagement. **It's about not just talking to but talking with individuals who identify with Black conservative thought. It requires us to ask probing questions, to challenge assumptions, and to seek out common values.** The dialogue should not be a platform primarily for proselytizing or pontificating but rather an environment where ideas can be exchanged, debated, and refined.

To engage constructively is to walk in another's shoes, even if just for a mile. We must remember that every individual's journey, including that of the Black conservative, deserves our respect and acknowledgment. This chapter has reminded us that the essence of empathetic engagement lies in listening with a heart open to understanding experiences that might be foreign to our own. **Building bridges** of communication is not just beneficial — it's essential for a cohesive society that values all of its constituents.

This approach will not only demystify Black conservative perspectives but also foster an environment where political and racial diversity is celebrated as a strength. Through informed dialogue, we can contribute to a broader understanding — and appreciation — of the rich tapestry of Black American political thought.

Nuanced Dialogue and Informed Debate

Promoting dialogue that honors the nuances of Black conservative thought is akin to laying a solid foundation for informed debate. The Bible says in Proverbs 27:17 that *"Iron sharpens iron, and one man sharpens another"* — through robust discourse, we refine each other's ideas and perspectives.

Throughout this chapter, our guiding light has been the spiritual maxim akin to "love thy neighbor." This principle undergirds **the need to create space for respectful understanding and collaboration between varying ideological stances within the Black community**. As we possess different gifts, like the parts of one body, we owe it to one another to nurture a professional yet compassionate environment where all voices can be heard and valued as potential collaborators.

Seeing Beyond the Surface

It is often in the simple acts of sharing stories and examples that we reveal the depths of our shared humanity. There is profound power in the individual narrative, which, when shared, commands attention and fosters empathy. By valuing each person's journey, particularly through the lens of faith and perseverance, we touch upon the very heart of relational growth and societal development.

Cherish each narrative with the reverence it deserves, for in doing so, we acknowledge the immeasurable worth of every person's experience. This is the essence of patriotism — not just the waving of a flag, but the upholding of one another's rights and stories under a common and united cause in the grand tapestry of a nation's history.

Engaging with Authority and Clarity

In moving forward, let us articulate our viewpoints with confidence and authority. **It is no longer acceptable to cowardly stand on the sidelines and passively accept a worldview that contradicts yours**; we must engage actively and wholeheartedly in the conversations that shape our society. This requires a level of clarity and resolution that leaves no room for misunderstanding. Assert your participation in the dialogue with the determination of someone who has not only witnessed the landscape but has toiled within it.

It is time to take action — to not just read and discuss but to embody the truths we have uncovered. Let today be the day you commit to engaging with different perspectives, to educating yourself further, and to contributing to a more holistic understanding of the diverse political thought within the Black community.

As we close this chapter, let it be the opening of countless discussions, the beginning of many journeys of understanding, and the inspiration for continuous growth and engagement in the varied and vibrant arena of Black conservatism. Let us walk forth with the valor of David, the wisdom of Solomon, and the understanding heart of Jesus that knows the true meaning of community and compassion.

Chapter Nine

The Evolving Narrative: Next-Generation Black Conservatives

I t was mid-afternoon as Michael found a quiet nook in the public library, the sun's persisting rays forcefully penetrating the lightly-dusted windows and laying a warm hand across the open pages of a book spread before him. The book was as much a balm as it was a source of profound reflection, stirring the embers of a passion that belied his young age. He was a standout figure, a young Black conservative, rare in his community, threading through the eye of a political needle that many had not dared to peer through.

The pages before him spoke of visionary leaders, mavericks who looked like him but preached a gospel that seemed foreign to the ears of his family. They spoke of empowerment, economic uplifting, and traditional values, and though the words resonated, they also isolated. It was the burden of being an anomaly, he thought. The quiet of the library allowed his mind to dance with the ideas, to sit in the silence and truly contemplate the trajectory of his own political involvement. His thoughts whispered of boardrooms and community centers, of podiums where his voice might one day echo the principles he was slowly making his own.

In the midst of silence and study, the faintest hum of life outside the library seeped through the walls — the distant laughter of children playing, the rhythmic thud of footsteps from passersby — each a testament to the world that awaited the fruits of his learning. He pictured himself there, amongst the people, championing the unvoiced concerns of his conservative kin. With each turn of the page, Michael saw himself not just as a member of his community but as a beacon of what could be, if only perspectives shifted, even slightly.

His foresight married entrepreneurship to activism, and his faith was the dowry. The scriptures had taught him of Joseph, a man sold into slavery, who arose to become the second most powerful in Egypt. In that Exodus story, Michael was inspired to learn that what may turn out initially bad can ultimately work out for his good after all. One of Michael's favorite Bible verses was Jeremiah 29:11 - "For I know the plans I have for you," declared the Lord, "plans to prosper you and not to harm you, plans to give you hope and a future." It was in this divine plan that Michael saw his own story reflected; a story still unfolding but certainly already written in the stars.

The ivory keys of his laptop broke the silence, a clarion call for the aspirations he was preparing to release into the ether. With each word typed, an absorbent mind downloaded the strategies that industry titans and faith leaders wove into the very fabric of his being. Michael knew that true change seemed impossible for him to enact on his own, but with faith as his guide, all things were possible.

Without lifting his gaze from the screen, he contemplated the possibility of his dreams, the change he might inspire. How would the emerging voices of Black conservative youth shape the turbulent political conversation and the shaky fabric of the nation? Could he prove to be the vessel through which those voices gained volume and strength?

Such were his musings when the assistant librarian passed by him, offering a smile of encouragement, a subtle yet tangible acknowledgment of the journey he was on. It was in her eyes, the spark of understanding, the recognition of a soul driven by a higher calling.

Following the past generations of his grandparents and ancestors, would he and those like him forge their own path, turning tides and upending expectations? Could the world adjust its lens to see the promise that lay in the growing reemergence of Black conservative thought?

A New Dawn for Black Conservatism

The landscape of American political thought is experiencing a seismic shift as a new generation of young Black conservatives emerges, challenging traditional narratives and reshaping the conversation around Black patriotism. Within these pages lies not a rebuke of the past but a meticulous navigation through the rich tapestry of Black conservatism, painting a portrait of a movement that is as resilient as it is misunderstood. We engage with forward-thinkers who are crafting an inclusive discourse that defies monolithic political characterizations and brings new vitality to the tenets of conservative philosophy.

The past decade has witnessed a growing crescendo in the chorus of Black voices who align with conservative principles. This uptick is not a mere anomaly but a renaissance of sorts — a deliberate and strategic realignment around policies that advocate for self-reliance, traditional family values, and economic freedom. To ignore the implications would be to disregard a critical component of the evolving Black American narrative. As this chapter unfolds, we will investigate how perceptions of Black conservatism are changing in the age of dynamic thinkers and maverick leaders, whose visions are steering the community through uncharted waters, similar to Moses and the Red Sea.

Anticipating the future trajectory of Black conservative political involvement in America provides not only a glimpse into the coming chapters of our nation's history but also **an opportunity for all political parties to engage in more nuanced and inclusive conversations**. This introspection requires both wisdom and discernment; it demands that we become attentive listeners to the echoes of the past as they inform our present and predict our future. We delve into the significance of this transformative period, exploring its potential to redefine the political arena and, by extension, the fabric of American society.

The vibrancy and diversity of thought within the emergent next generation of Black conservatives cannot be overstated. Their voices, rich with the enthusiasm of youth and the sobering realities of their unique American experiences, are the new speakers of intellectual conservatism. By understanding, nurturing and incorporating these voices into the political conversation, we can achieve a richer, more complete picture of Black patriotism and its role within the grand American experiment.

These modern conservative voices are not simply echoes of the past but represent a sophisticated synthesis of age-old values and contemporary societal concerns. Their advocacy is not a monolith; it manifests in diverse areas such as fiscal responsibility, educational reform, and cultural pride, underscored by a shared valorization of individual liberty, respect for law & order, and self-reliance.

Spreading the Message of Black Conservative Philosophy Today

This modern cohort of Black conservatives leverages innovative platforms to voice their opinions, reforming how their stance is perceived and heard. The use of social media, podcasts, and blogs has democratized their reach, allowing for a broader, more engaged audience. Unlike in previous eras, where gatekeepers might have limited exposure, these platforms provide a direct line to the public. **The messaging, often grounded in personal experience, carries undertones of empowerment rather than the subservience that critics of conservatism have historically alleged.** There's a palpable sense that these conservatives are the architects of their narratives, not mere inheritors of a predetermined doctrine.

Spiritual Foundations in Modern Black Conservatism

The spiritual element remains integral to the next generation of the Black conservative movement. The teachings of sacred texts continue to serve as moral compasses, guiding leaders and their communities toward values such as integrity, family, and compassion. For instance, the advocacy for school choice, a prominent issue among Black conservatives, can be linked to the deeply religious notion of stewardship — parents taking responsibility for the education and moral upbringing of their children. This coupling of spiritual wisdom with policy initiatives represents a harnessing of faith to impact the temporal and fallen world, a tradition that has long imbued Black political engagement with its resolute strength.

Continuing the Legacy to Call for Entrepreneurial Action

Moreover, this era of Black conservatism prominently features a clarion call for entrepreneurship and economic self-sufficiency. Harboring the belief that economic empowerment is key to advancing their communities, these conservative leaders often frame business ownership not just as a means to wealth, but as a catalyst for autonomy and respect. They inspire action, urging their communities to rise above systemic challenges through innovation, hard work, and prudent financial stewardship. Their rhetoric elevates these narratives from mere concepts into actionable paths, equipping individuals with the vision and verve to transform their circumstances.

The Confluence of Expertise and Real-World Examples

Backed by expertise in various fields, these new leaders do not shy away from highlighting real-world examples of successful conservative policies. By providing practical illustrations — from the revitalization of neglected neighborhoods through community-led initiatives to the bolstering of local economies via deregulation — they offer a clear, tangible stance that resonates with everyday aspirations. This effective blend of lived experience and professional acumen gives credibility to their arguments, sowing seeds of consideration even amongst skeptics.

Inclusive and Personal Dialogues

In this dialogue, the tone is neither aloof nor combative, but rather warm and personal, inviting listeners into a conversation about shared values and common goals. By sharing their own journeys and entrepreneurial endeavors, these leaders forge a bond with their audience, underscoring the universal desire for dignity and achievement. It's through these narratives that Black conservatism becomes not just an ideology, but a collective story of aspiration and resilience that is becoming more and more attractive to those who have been taken for granted on the other side of the aisle.

A Simple, Persuasive and Instructive Narrative

Their stories are persuasive, illustrating the potential for success and fulfillment when one aligns with conservative principles. The instructive voice of these leaders guides the audience toward a deeper understanding of how political theory translates into real-life benefits. They are adept at elucidating complex economic theories or interpreting legislative language in ways that are simple to understand yet illuminate the practical advantages for individuals, families and communities alike.

Evolution Through Diversity of Discourse

The richness of this modern discourse is amplified by the embrace of a broad spectrum of insight, ranging from theology to politics, to economics. This interweaving of disciplines presents a comprehensive worldview that is as erudite as it is accessible. It's through this multiplicity of perspectives and the willingness to engage with complex subjects, that Black conservatism in America continues an evolution marked by diversity, intellectualism, and relevance.

As these new voices rise, they remind us that conservatism within the Black community is not fixed; it is constantly being redefined by the experiences and insights of its proponents. With this understanding, we are better equipped to appreciate the complexity and the distinctiveness of the next generation of Black conservatives. Their voices contribute to a more nuanced and vibrant tapestry of political thought, elevating the dialogue and shaping the blueprint for future policy and community engagement.

Bridging Business and Community

These young innovators are not content with siloed success within echo chambers of people that think like them; instead, they seek avenues where economic prosperity can intersect with communal uplift across all people, whether they share the same views or not. Much like business leaders who understand the symbiosis between thriving enterprises and the communities they serve, these thought leaders advocate for policies and programs that benefit the broader Black community while upholding conservative values. Championing school choice, advocating for enterprise zones in economically depressed areas, and pressing for reforms that enhance personal responsibility are just a few of the practical strategies they employ to achieve these ends that impact all people, regardless of their background or political affiliation.

Empowering Engagement

The future of Black conservatism is being prepared by engaging with the youth now, leading them to a political philosophy that resonates with their aspirations. Invitations to participate in discourse, to voice opinions, and to engage actively in shaping policy are extended in a manner that excites and motivates the next generation by including them to the table.

Show, Don't Tell

The principles of "show, don't tell" resonate deeply with this new wave of conservatives, who wield the power of example as their most persuasive tool. By showcasing success stories and creating templates for replication, these emerging leaders provide tangible blueprints for others to follow. Their philosophy transcends mere rhetoric; it takes the form of community centers that foster entrepreneurship, mentorship programs that cultivate leadership, and social initiatives that reinforce traditional family values.

The Projection of Young Conservative Valor

Amidst a climate that sometimes views conservative principles with skepticism, young Black conservatives stand **ready to challenge the status quo**. With entrepreneurial spirit and resolve, they are rewriting the narrative, proving that conservative values can be the engine driving innovation and economic mobility. For these young minds, self-reliance and capitalist ideals are the building blocks for creating and seizing opportunities, underscoring the belief that individual tenacity can coexist with community upliftment.

Wisdom Through Relatable Narratives

By sharing relatable personal stories, young Black conservatives form a **bridge of connectivity** with their peers and elders. They understand the importance of personal narratives in illustrating their visions for the future. Through these accounts, they evoke a sense of camaraderie, uniting like-minded individuals in a collective journey towards societal progress without sacrificing personal beliefs or cultural heritage.

Engaging Debate with Conviction

In the company of the next generation, political debate gains a reju-
venated vigor. **Their ability to articulate their views with confidence, backed by solid arguments and an understanding of
historical and economic contexts, is motivating a reevaluation
of preconceived notions.** Their discourse is not only assertive but
also diplomatic, inviting conversations that challenge and expand ideological boundaries.

A Resounding Clarion Call

The voices of next-generation Black conservatives are akin to a clarion call, urging not only the Black community but also the broader American public to reconsider the multiplicity of Black political
thought. They beckon us to acknowledge the undercurrents shaping
America's political future, emphasizing the importance of their place
at the table. This next generation crafts a vision for conservatism that is
not only informed by past wisdom but also tailor-fit for contemporary
challenges. **Without their perspectives, any narrative on Black
conservatism is incomplete, lacking the dynamism and diversity
that these young minds offer.**

A Call to Action

**The imperative now is to listen, incorporate, and amplify these
voices. Engagement with emerging Black conservative youth
should not be an afterthought but a priority. Those invested in the future of conservatism must act with intention to**

mentor and prop up these individuals, providing them with platforms to express their thoughts and tools to implement their ideas. Their narrative will undoubtedly shape the trajectory of Black conservative contributions to the nation's discourse, signaling an era of transformation and a redefinition of what it means to be a conservative, let alone a Black conservative, in America.

Engagement and Representation

Looking towards the horizon, one can confidently **anticipate an increase in the political involvement of such young Black conservatives**. It's not just about numbers; it's about the quality of engagement and the depth of representation. As the voices from this community gain volume and clarity, their influence is poised to expand in political arenas nationwide, heralding a more nuanced dialogue on national issues. The resolve and ingenuity that have long characterized the Black community are finding new outlets in conservative thought, offering a compelling narrative of empowerment and self-determination.

Nurturing the Next Generation

Acknowledging and nurturing the voices of young, emerging Black conservatives is tantamount to curating a future rich in diverse leadership. This entails **creating platforms for dialogue,** fostering mentorship programs, and most importantly, listening. There is wisdom in Proverbs 22:6, which teaches us to *"train up a child in the way he should go, and when he is old, he will not depart from it."* By imbuing young conservatives with not just political ideologies but also a strong moral foundation, we equip them to navigate and shape the political tides of the future.

The burgeoning energy of the youth is not to be underestimated. Their passion, when channeled through the prisms of spirituality and thoughtful conservatism, can pioneer innovative solutions to age-old dilemmas. Their contribution promises to add depth and color to the broad spectrum of Black political thought, turning the page for the next chapter in American political history, equipped with solutions that get the right results for communities regardless of color. These new leaders are the ones that the Republican Party is looking to embrace and to include towards its movement to position America back to economic and moral greatness among the world's nations.

Cultivating Informed Discourse and Strategic Alliances

To cultivate a movement that endures and inspires, we must engage in informed discourse that bridges gaps and fosters understanding across differing viewpoints. This is a movement enriched by diversity of thought, and it thrives through strategic alliances that transcend mere political affiliations. By invoking the wisdom of Ecclesiastes 4:12 - *"A person standing alone can be attacked and defeated, but two can stand back-to-back and conquer. Three are even better, for a triple-braided cord is not easily broken."* - we are reminded of the enduring strength found in unity.

A Call to Resolute Action

The journey ahead calls for resolute action. **It beckons Black conservatives to rise with courage, armed with the wisdom of our ancestors and the innovative spirit of our youth.** It is time to solidify our place in the annals of political history, shaping policies and perceptions alike. Let us therefore approach the future with both reverence and boldness, committed to a vision that upholds the best of our heritage while forging new paths for prosperity, righteousness and justice. This evolving narrative is not just a chapter in a book; it is the ongoing story of a people, forever striving, forever ascending to the heights of their God-given potential.

Chapter Ten

A Seat at the Table: Cementing Black Conservatism in America's Future

T he oak-paneled room was a testament to tradition, mahogany desks and leather-bound tomes lining the shelf, dust particles performing a lazy ballet in the sun-streaked silence. Here, Solomon, a policy advisor, sat in contemplative repose. His mind, however, was not on the books that had guided him thus far, but on the heavenly call for wisdom to address the recognition of Black conservatives in a political landscape that felt as vast and unmapped as the sea.

He thought of Proverbs 11:14, *"without wise leadership, a nation falls; there is safety in having many advisers,"* and considered how the inclusion of Black conservative voices could indeed make the political process safer, richer, more attuned to echoes of diversity. The sunlight warming his hands on the desk traveled with a regal slow-motion across the room that felt both timely and significant.

A tapping at his door and his train of thought, delicate as the intricacies of a spider's web, was broken. A colleague entered, embodying the enthusiastic determination of the youth, a fresh intern armed with ideas and questions, a reminder of the future that they were shaping. "How do we make sure everyone is represented?" she asked.

"Like the human body, politics needs every part to function effectively," Solomon responded, as if reciting a scripture from his mental anthology. His advice was a seamless blend of spiritual and secular, of faith informing duty. There was a unity in his perspective that transcended mere political agendas; it spoke of a moral imperative of togetherness and shared respect. "We listen, we advocate, and we act," he stated, his voice a beacon in an oft-stormy sea.

They looked together at the bustling city through the office window, pondering over the chaotic order of cars and people beneath them. Their collective gaze returned to the task that lingered heavily in the air – shaping a world better equipped for conversations yet to be had, for debates yet to be won, for inclusivity yet to be embraced.

Solomon sat back in his chair and his eyes returned to his Bible, his heart seeking guidance from the divine, the ancient verses speaking to contemporary conundrums. A strategic combination of the lessons from theology, his understanding of politics, and his past experiences in economics formed the foundation of his resolve. He imagined a path forward, one where the cacophony of political discourse was harmonized by the inclusion of every voice, where wisdom and practicality dictated recognition over majority.

As the intern left, inspired and motivated by Solomon's quiet confidence, he turned to view the setting sun, the day's end reminding him of the work still left to be done. His thoughts once again reached towards the horizon of possibility, where every challenge faced with faith could find its answer, where every counsel taken in the spirit of unity could build a bridge towards understanding.

And as the night crept over the bustling city, ushering in the stars like watchful guardians of the toils below, a thought hung in the air, unspoken yet resonant, leaving one to wonder: How might the lessons of the past enrich the paths we pave for the future, and in what ways can wisdom of the ancients illuminate our modern quests for political inclusion?

The Untapped Voices of Progress

American democracy is built on a foundation of diverse thought, yet the narrative around Black political ideology has often been painted in monochrome. What has been traditionally underrepresented in the historical tableau of American conservatism is the substantive role that Black conservative voices have and should continue to play in shaping the nation's future. The recognition and integration of these voices are not mere token gestures; they are crucial to the enrichment and the authenticity of American political discourse.

The political sphere demands a multiplicity of voices to thrive. For Black conservatism to be genuinely recognized, it must be acknowledged not as an outlier but as a vital ingredient in the melting pot of American political ideology. This acknowledgment comes from an understanding that Black conservatism is not a monolith; it presents a spectrum of thought as diverse as the community it represents. Affirming its necessity is the first step toward disrupting a one-dimensional view of Black political identity.

Envisioning a well-informed political landscape begins with the acceptance that Black conservative perspectives can offer enriching insights shaped by unique experiences, as well as policies that actually get results to better the communities that they serve, regardless of race. Their inclusion does not simply add more voices to the choir but brings different melodies, rich harmonies, and a symphony of ideas that reflect the broader society. It is about bridging cultural gaps and lending clarity to misunderstood aspects of Black conservatism, allowing for a more "whole" approach to governance and policy-making.

It is essential, too, to remember that this is about more than political theory; it is about the living, breathing individuals who carry these ideals. Real-world experiences illustrate the relevance and importance of Black conservative voices. Personal anecdotes not only provide a window into the lives that endorse these views but also demonstrate how they have been instrumental in driving forward the principles they believe in — principles which often align with the core values of spiritual teachings like integrity, responsibility, and community.

In this landscape, however, being recognized and included is not the end goal — it is the beginning of a new chapter in American history. Acknowledging Black conservatism's role demands that it is met with a seat at the table, where decisions are made, and futures are shaped. The entrepreneurial spirit of action and perseverance underscores the approach Black conservatives often take, advocating for economic freedom, personal responsibility, and limited government intervention as means to achieve success.

By engaging with this chapter, readers will grasp that the Black conservative movement is about more than political alignment; it is a profound expression of patriotism and love for America. A patriotism that should be understood, respected, and incorporated into the national consciousness for a truer depiction of the ideological diversity that exists within America. This chapter serves as both a learning objective and a rallying cry for inclusion, balance, and mutual respect in the unfolding story of American conservatism. It challenges readers to embrace the complexities of the political landscape and to appreciate the broad range of insights that can result from such inclusivity.

In this crucible of political thought, it is not enough to simply envision; we must act. The path to a future where the full spectrum of Black political ideology is not only acknowledged but also revered is one that requires dedication, advocacy, and a steadfast resolve. It calls for setting aside preconceived notions and engaging in open dialogue with those who champion these conservative values. Through learning, understanding, and respecting the multitude of voices that constitute the fabric of Black conservatism, we carve a path to a more just and representative future.

In the mosaic of American political thought, every constituent part adds depth and nuance to the overall picture. The necessity of Black conservative recognition in the political sphere is fundamental not only to the principle of genuine representation but also to the full expression of America's democratic ideology. Acknowledging Black conservatism is more than an act of inclusivity; it is a commitment to understanding the diverse ways in which individuals interpret and respond to the societal structures around them. As Scripture teaches us, "In the multitude of counselors there is safety" (Proverbs 11:14). This wisdom underlines the importance of multiple voices in the decision-making process to ensure that policies are well-rounded and considerate of all those under their purview.

Black conservatism is far from a monolith, and its vast array of philosophies and priorities reflects the heterogeneity of Black America itself. Recognizing this faction within the Black community does more than just broaden the political spectrum; it dismantles the stereotype that Black identity is tied to a single political affiliation. **This one recognition provokes a discourse that can reshape coalitions and strategies, influencing the political process at every level.** Moreover, those with a conservative outlook hold dear principles such as fiscal responsibility, limited government, and individual liberties — concepts that resonate with a broad swath of the American electorate, irrespective of race, from Wall Street to Main Street, from the inner cities to the suburbs, from the rural countryside to the bustling metropolis, from vocational schools to the Ivy League.

The acknowledgement of Black conservatives also serves as a contrarian force to push the boundaries of political dialogue, fostering a more rigorous ideological contest. **Just as in business, where competition spurs innovation and excellence, in politics, exposure to competing views encourages parties to refine their platforms and adapt to a changing electorate.** Diverse perspectives ensure that policy solutions are both innovative and comprehensive. The Bible's exhortation to "*As iron sharpens iron, so one person sharpens another*" (Proverbs 27:17) aligns with the political domain, suggesting that through challenging each other's beliefs, individuals, and by extension, parties, improve their character and capability to serve the community.

Incorporating and valuing Black conservative voices is also a nod towards authenticity in political representation. **The presence of Black conservative leaders and thinkers in visible and influential positions creates a more accurate portrayal of Black political agency. It reminds us that public service and governance are not** the exclusive realms of any one group. Politics at its best is about giving life to the voices of the people; when we acknowledge the multiple political identities within the Black community, we encourage a fuller participation in the democratic process.

This recognition must also extend to the grassroots level, where the political establishment tends to overlook Black conservative opinions. **It's about recognizing the value of the small business owner, the high school principal, the religious leader, and the community advocates who champion policies aligned with conservative values. Their lived experiences and contributions provide tangible proof of the efficacy of conservative principles in practice.** A politics devoid of their influence would be an incomplete picture of America's social fabric, denying the country the benefit of their profound insights and entrepreneurial spirit.

For Black conservatism to be rightly recognized, there must be a concerted effort to create pathways for individuals who hold these values to enter and influence the public sphere. This could manifest in a number of ways – through mentorship programs, platforms to introduce your voices to local and national audiences, networking events, or intentional outreach activities to engage with conservative communities. **Failure to do so not only sidelines a critical voice but also impoverishes the decision-making process, leading to policies that may not fully address the needs of all citizens.**

Bridging Divides with Inclusive Dialogue

The act of silencing, marginalizing or even canceling any political voice only serves to fracture society, creating schisms that hinder our collective progress. By extending a seat at the table to

Black conservatives, one extends a hand across the aisle. **History has shown us that great leaps forward often occur when seemingly disparate parties find common ground and form strategic alliances and partnerships.** Psalm 133:1 reads, *"How good and pleasant it is when God's people live together in unity!"* Thus, the inclusion of diverse ideologies is more than a political courtesy — it is a profound move towards unity without uniformity, facilitating an environment where all citizens can coexist and love one another and their country, even if they think, believe and vote differently than each other sometimes.

Fostering Mentorship and Community Building

Inclusion does not merely add voices to the conversation; it creates leaders and mentors within the political sphere. Black conservative role models offer tangible proof that adherence to conservative values can coexist with a strong Black identity. In sharing their journeys, they become beacons for the next generation, guiding them towards an understanding that their options are not limited to a single ideological path. This personal touch fosters a warmer political climate where young Black Americans feel seen, supported, and empowered to pursue their individual aspirations.

Catalyzing Political Engagement Through Authentic Representation

Seeing oneself reflected in politics is a powerful motivator for civic engagement. When Black conservative voices are not just included but actively engaged, **it inspires participation from those who share these views but may have felt previously unrep-**

resented. This engagement, in turn, lends itself to a more diverse and dynamic electorate that is instrumental in shaping policies that align with the values of a broader population. Encouraging the heart of democracy, this effect underpins the vitality and longevity of our political institutions and ensures that they are truly representative of all citizens.

A Welcoming Table for All (Conservative) Voices

The political landscape of tomorrow must be one where Black conservatism is not just an observer but a significant contributor to the national dialogue. Envision a political sphere where the counsel of Black conservatives is actively sought and valued, where their insights are considered an essential component of the policy-making process. A future that values diverse perspectives ensures a richer tapestry of ideas, fostering policies that are more reflective of the nation's full demographic landscape.

Towards a More Inclusive Tomorrow

As we look towards the future, we envision an America that proudly upholds its founding principles of liberty and justice for all, with a clear understanding that these principles must be applied irrespective of political affiliation. **The inclusion of Black conservative voices in the grand narrative of American progress is not merely a sign of political maturity; it is an embodiment of the nation's core belief in the unalienable rights of all its citizens.** Each perspective added to the national conversation is a step closer to a society where equality and prosperity are not aspirations but realities for all.

Ushering in this era of enlightenment and inclusivity requires dedication, dialogue, and an unyielding commitment to fairness. **It asks that we embrace complexity, challenge prejudices, and celebrate diversity in thought. This is the path to a well-informed and emotionally intelligent nation**; a place where the integrity of the American promise shines bright for every citizen, and where the echoes of liberty harmonize with the voices of its diverse populace.

Vision for an Inclusive Future

A robust and inclusive political landscape where diverse Black narratives are integrated is the goal we must aspire to achieve. In business as in politics, ignoring a subset of perspectives can lead to incomplete strategies; embracing them, however, paves the way toward innovation and growth. As we look to the future, **let us be inspired to forge a path where dialogue includes the broad spectrum of Black conservatism,** engaging with respect, humility, empathy, and the collective wisdom of all community members. We do not predict the future so much as we participate in its creation, mindful of our responsibility to guide it towards more inclusive, informed deliberation.

The quest to demystify Black conservatism has been both intricate and illuminating. The perspectives and historical insights shared herein are seeds planted in the rich soil of our collective consciousness, which, when nurtured by dialogue and understanding, will yield a harvest of progress and unity. By engaging with these ideas, you are now better equipped to advocate for a more representative discourse and to contribute meaningfully to the shaping of America's political future.

As we move forward, let the values of respect, integration, and mutual recognition guide us, much as the wise master builders of old would lay a strong and inclusive foundation. The future beckons with a promise, and it is up to each one of us to respond with intention and conviction. Let us, therefore, proceed with the steadfastness of those who have gone before us, carrying the baton of liberty and justice for all, and ever mindful of the significance of a seat at the table.

Final Marching Orders for Black Conservatism

As we draw the curtains on this expedition through the rich tapestry of Black Conservative thought, it is worthwhile to contemplate the influence and significance of such a journey. Not merely as an intellectual pursuit, but as a real-world blueprint for the robust engagement of political ideals in our daily lives.

The lessons within these pages reach far beyond the confines of theoretical discourse, empowering us to navigate the political landscape with both wisdom and grace. Guided by the call to stewardship, let us consider how the insights we've gleaned can be channeled into fostering growth, not only in our personal ambitions but also in our families, communities and beyond.

Recalling the main thoroughfares we have journeyed through, we have encountered the historical underpinnings of Black Conservatism, its debates, its champions, and its vibrant lifeblood that pulses with diversity of thought. Each chapter has laid another stone on the path of understanding, enabling us to traverse the distance between perception and reality, between past histories and future potentialities.

In applying this knowledge, you are encouraged to engage in your own spheres of influence with renewed perspective. Whether as students, entrepreneurs, or future political leaders, the strategies and values explored within these covers can serve as a compass for those striving to enact change through conservative principles anchored in tradition, morality, and an entrepreneurial spirit.

While we have illuminated much in these pages, let us acknowledge the terrains yet unexplored. The canvas of Black Conservatism, rich and varied, demands a continual quest for deeper comprehension, an ever-evolving dialogue that beckons new voices and perspectives.

To heed this call to action, **start by initiating conversations that challenge misconceptions, advocate for educational curricula that include a more varied spectrum of Black political thought, or support institutions and leaders who embody these values. Let us uplift and amplify the voices within the Black Conservative movement that are often overlooked or silenced.**

Despite my humble attempt at diligence on this subject, we must recognize that this work is only an introduction to an expansive field. Further research, discourse, and introspection are needed to further unravel the nuances that remain concealed within this topic, for every answered query paves the way for a dozen new inquisitions.

I charge you, dear reader, to not only absorb but to imbibe the essence of what you have learned. Let it beckon you toward action and inspire you to forge paths where before there were none. May your ventures reflect not only the acumen gathered but also the heart with which it was shared.

In the spirit of moving forward with this newfound knowledge, I leave you with a quote that encapsulates the enduring power of ideas and the potential within every individual to effect meaningful change:

"The function of education is to teach one to think intensively and to think critically. Intelligence plus character – that is the goal of true education."

– Dr. Martin Luther King Jr.

May this book not only educate but instill within you a character that aspires to uphold conservative values, intertwines debate with empathy, and champions the causes, aspirations and dreams of American individuals, families, and communities nationwide as one nation, indivisible, with liberty and justice for all.

God bless you and God bless America.

About the Author

What is most important to Philip Blackett and what truly forms his identity is his relationship with his Lord and Savior Jesus Christ. Philip's mission for the rest of his life is to Grow God's People, Grow God's Businesses, and Grow God's Kingdom as a good and faithful steward of all God has entrusted him, while having a positive influence on all who he encounters each day as a Kingdom Man.

Professionally speaking, Philip is passionate about helping entrepreneurs and small business owners grow their dream businesses, while utilizing his skillset in sales, marketing and business development. Previously, Philip served as President of Cemetery Services, Inc., a seven-figure business he bought based in the Greater Boston area. It was "his pleasure" to also serve as a Manager for a Chick-Fil-A restaurant.

At FedEx, Philip previously provided support to several senior Marketing executives (including the current CEO) as a Senior Communications Specialist after working on its Corporate Social Responsibility team. Before FedEx, Philip advised investors on Wall Street in New York City as an Equity Research Analyst for Goldman Sachs, where he helped recommend investments in over 100 publicly traded companies across ten industries.

Regarding his education, Philip graduated from the Southern Baptist Theological Seminary with his Masters of Divinity (M.Div) degree with a concentration in Great Commission Studies. He also earned his MBA from Harvard Business School. In college, Philip graduated from the University of North Carolina at Chapel Hill as a Morehead-Cain Scholar, majoring in Political Science and Economics.

Philip is a Life Member of Alpha Phi Alpha Fraternity, Inc. When he is not actively fulfilling his mission, Philip enjoys reading, watching sports, and raising his twin daughters, Sofia and Elizabeth, with his wife Mayra.

Books by Philip

Disagree without Disrespect: How to Respectfully Debate with Those who Think, Believe and Vote Differently than You

Future-Proof: How to Adopt and Master Artificial Intelligence (A.I.) to Secure Your Job and Career

The Unfair Advantage: How Small Business Owners can Use Artificial Intelligence (A.I.) to Boost Sales, Outsmart the Competition and Grow their Dream Businesses without Breaking the Bank

Jesus over Black: How My Faith Transformed Me into a Conservative within the Black Community

Maverick Lineage: What I Learned about Black Conservatism in America

Bridging the GOP Gap: How the Republican Party can Win Over African American Voters with Inclusivity and Trust without Compromising Values

Connect with Philip

f

facebook.com/PhilipBlackettFB

𝕏

twitter.com/PhilipBlackett

in

linkedin.com/in/philipblackett

◯

instagram.com/philipblackett

▶

youtube.com/@PhilipBlackett

♪

tiktok.com/@pblackett

Facebook:
https://www.facebook.com/PhilipBlackettFB
X (Twitter):
https://twitter.com/PhilipBlackett
LinkedIn:
https://www.linkedin.com/in/philipblackett
Instagram:
https://instagram.com/philipblackett
YouTube:
https://www.youtube.com/@PhilipBlackett
TikTok:
https://www.tiktok.com/@pblackett
Blog:
https://www.PhilipBlackett.com

www.ingramcontent.com/pod-product-compliance
Lightning Source LLC
Chambersburg PA
CBHW022058020426
42335CB00012B/732